A JOURNAL OF CONTEMPORARY WRITING

IRISH PAGES
DUILLÍ ÉIREANN

IRISH PAGES is a biannual journal, edited in Belfast and publishing, in equal measure, writing from Ireland and overseas. It appears at the end of each six month period.

Its policy is to publish poetry, short fiction, essays, creative non-fiction, memoir, essay reviews, nature-writing, translated work, literary journalism, and other autobiographical, historical, religious and scientific writing of literary distinction. There are no standard reviews or narrowly academic articles. Irish-language and Scots writing are published in the original, with English translations or glosses. IRISH PAGES is a non-partisan, non-sectarian, culturally ecumenical, and wholly independent journal. It endorses no political outlook or cultural tradition, and has no editorial position on the constitutional question. Its title refers to the island of Ireland in a purely apolitical and geographic sense, in the same manner of The Church of Ireland or the Irish Sea.

The sole criteria for inclusion in the journal are the distinction of the writing and the integrity of the individual voice. Equal editorial attention will be given to established, emergent and new writers.

The views expressed in IRISH PAGES are not necessarily those of the Editors. The journal is published by Irish Pages Ltd, a non-profit organization.

Submissions, by post only, are welcome but must be accompanied by return postage or an international reply coupon. No self-addressed envelope is required. Reporting time is nine months. If work is accepted, an electronic copy may be requested.

Your subscription is essential to the independence and survival of the journal. Subscription rates are £24stg/€36/$72 for one year. Visit our website at www.irishpages.org for a subscription form or to order online. Credit cards are welcome.

IRISH PAGES
129 Ormeau Road
Belfast BT7 1SH

Advisory Board
William Crawley
Manfred McDowell
Ruth Carr
Bernard O'Donoghue
Noel Russell
Daniel Tobin

Legal Advice: Elliott Duffy Garrett, Belfast

IRISH PAGES is set in 12/14.5 Monotype Perpetua and printed in Glasgow by Bell & Bain.

This issue has been generously funded by Creative Scotland, and the Arts Councils of Northern and Southern Ireland.

Copyright remains with IRISH PAGES and the authors. All rights reserved.
No reproduction, copy or transmission, in whole or part, may be made without written permission.

ISBN 978-1-7390902-0-3

IRISH PAGES

CHRIS AGEE, *Editor*

KATHLEEN JAMIE, *Scottish Editor*

DON PATERSON & NIALL CAMPBELL, *Guest Editors*

RÓISÍN COSTELLO, *Irish Language Editor*

MEG BATEMAN, *Scottish Gaelic Editor*

JACOB AGEE, *Managing Editor*

RUTH CARR, STEPHEN DORNAN & RUTH PADEL, *Contributing Editors*

ALANNAH MILLAR (Scotland)
CASSIA BLONDELOT (Ireland)
Editorial Assistants

EDITED IN IRELAND & SCOTLAND
VOLUME 12, NUMBER 2

"These beginnings explain why, in contrast to so many other small nationalities, Scots don't pose as an 'ethnicity'. That great European, Hubert Butler of Kilkenny, once wrote about a conference seeking to soothe the Troubles that 'the Forum failed… but left a lingering sweetness in the air. The desire for unity and harmony is something like the desire to sleep.'"

Neal Ascherson

IRISH PAGES
DUILLÍ ÉIREANN

VOLUME 12, NUMBER 2

CONTENTS

Scotland

STANDS SCOTLAND WHERE IT DID?

Foreword	11	Kathleen Jamie & Don Paterson
Defeated But Never Conquered?	16	Neal Ascherson
At Achnabreac	24	Dougie Strang
Two Minutes' Pandemonium	29	Colin Bramwell
Truth-window	37	Kate Molleson
Weekend At Bernie's: *A Survey of Recent Scottish Theatre*	44	David Greig
An Ecology of Haunting: Re-forming a Future from Scotland's Past	52	Margaret Elphinstone
Where Stands Gaelic Literature?	59	Peter Mackay
The Critical State of Scottish Book Reviewing	65	Rosemary Goring
D'où Venons-Nous / Que Sommes-Nous / Où Allons-Nous	72	Don Paterson
All the Rage: Reflections on a Fractious Decade for Live Poetry in Scotland	81	Jenny Lindsay
Late to the Party	88	Stuart Kelly

A Distant Prospect	97	James Campbell
Recovery	104	James Robertson
Losing Our Religion	111	Fraser MacDonald
Notes on a Scottish Feminist Aesthetic	117	Catriona McAra
Stories-so-far	124	Amanda Thomson
In Search of Sarmatia: on the Trail of Johannes Bobrowski	133	David Wheatley

NEW SCOTTISH POETS

Foreword	141	Niall Campbell
When I See the Stars in the Night Sky	143	Marjorie Lotfi
Kaieteur Falls	144	Roshni Gallagher
Autumn Geese at Montrose Basin	145	Taylor Strickland
Defence of the Realm	146	Sam Tongue
John Knox, Dying	147	Michael Grieve
Delhi, Night	148	Medha Singh
Maricruz Paredes	149	Colin Bramwell
"You Had a Daughter. I Feel Sad for Her."	151	Nuala Watt
The Ringing Stone	153	Tarn MacArthur
Salvaging	154	Tim Tim Cheng
If I Couldn't Sleep in the Granary	155	Patrick Romero McCafferty
Fieldnotes in Lake District Mist	156	Alycia Pirmohamed
Did You Always Have a Passion for Staying Very Still?	157	Iona Lee

Venery, Off Range Road 134, East of Vegreville, Alberta	158	Patrick James Errington
Death to My Hometown	160	Harry Ledgerwood
Swallowing the Anchor	162	Siún Carden
from Acts of Joy	163	Will Barnard

A SOUNDING BOX

Forkit Tongue	167	Brian Holton
Cleachdadh An Neach-Chùil	172	Niall O'Gallagher
Two Diptychs	174	David Kinloch
Interior With Interior	183	David Wheatley
Airdrie	186	Rob McClure
City Snowprints, 2018	188	Ryan Van Winkle
An Island Speaks to its Castle	190	Morag Smith
Those Launds	192	Finola Scott
To Make Your Very Own Dùn	194	Alec Finlay with Ken Cockburn

FROM THE SCOTTISH ARCHIVE

Scottish Culture and the End of Britain (2002)	199	Angus Calder

The Patron of This Issue

SCOTTISH POETRY LIBRARY
EDINBURGH

FRIENDS AND SUPPORTERS OF *IRISH PAGES*

Anonymous (Glasgow)
Gerry Bell
Graham Benson
Lucy Brennan
Vincent Browne
Paddy and Feena Bushe
John Cassidy
Manus Charleton
Jenny Cleland
Charles Coventry
Maggie Dalton
Joan Dargan
Donnell and Alison Deeny
Joe and Geraldine Duffy
Jeannie Farr
Gandolfi Fish (Glasgow)
Brendan Flynn
Elliot Duffy Garrett
Jack Gillespie
André Gumuchdjian
Joseph M Hassett
Philip Haughey
Marie Heaney
Kenneth Irvine

Celeste King
John Liddy
Brian Mac Call
Celine Mac Intyre
Enda McDonough
Manfred McDowell
Robert McDowell
John McGinley
John McMahon
Colette Ní Ghallchóir
Patricia Ní Ivor
Gordon Peake
Peter Power-Hynes
Joe Prendergast
Gillian Reynolds
William Reynolds
Carolyn Richardson
Tony Skelton
Anne Smith
Alex Stafford
Timothy Vignoles
Bret Walker
David Woods

Subscribe / donate / purchase books online at www.irishpages.org

STANDS SCOTLAND WHERE IT DID?

THE SCOTTISH PARLIAMENT
EDINBURGH

Ten years after the Independence Referendum, Irish Pages *asks Scottish writers of distinction to think about their country, and take stock of the current state of its culture and polity, language and literature, ecology and environment, while a specially curated selection of Scotland's emerging poets offer a younger perspective. How will Scotland fare in an era of momentous and unpredictable political change? Stands Scotland where it did?*

Kathleen Jamie, Scotland's Makar (2021–2024)

FOREWORD

Kathleen Jamie & Don Paterson

In rest we gather strength.

Late 2023, and the two present editors found themselves in a not-unfamiliar situation: happed up in an Edinburgh café, whining over the state of Scottish letters, culture and political discourse. It occurred to us that the 10-year anniversary of the Scottish Independence Referendum was nigh; it had to occur to us, because no one seemed to be talking about it. It was a cause most Scottish artists and writers had supported. Ten years since that extraordinary excitement; ten years since our country seemed transformed into an "open air university", as folk educated themselves about Scottish history, their place in the UK and the constitutional details of the Union; we were suddenly a nation of experts. Ten years since the great YES marches, too big for even the BBC to fail to report. Ten years since all the online hilarity, and the failed attempts to impute an anti-English agenda to an almost overwhelmingly Anglophile, diverse and inclusive movement with many English-born supporters. And ten years since a propaganda war, the likes of which we had never known before. We were naïve to think that the might of the UK state machine, with all its broadcasters, newspapers, media outlets and whispering campaigns, would not be directed against us. Some of us were lifelong supporters of the independence cause; many more were newcomers to the idea. But we were still UK citizens, and used to the principle of reasonably disinterested balance being applied to the way our words and actions were reported. But lord, did we wise up quickly. OK. So *this* was how states acted when they felt threatened.

The state denied it, of course, denied all its misinformation, veiled threat and gaslighting. Many of our (many) Unionist friends, in both Scotland and England, denied it too, because the luxury of occupying the status quo blinded them to their own British nationalism. It was an irreconcilable difference of perspective. We could not convince them that nationalism is just the neutral state of every nation which believes in its own borders, that "independence is normal", that patriotism need have no implication of blood and soil. No, nationalism was our fever and illness alone. Though the threat of our leaving the UK suddenly got Scotland noticed. Celebs and politicians from throughout the UK begged us in the press. *We hear you. But we love coming up north for the Festival. Could you please not abandon us? We need your votes in Westminster to save us from the Tories. You won't be able to feed yourselves. You won't have any friends of our own. We'll keep all your stuff.* (All except the UK's Trident nuclear missiles. Apparently we'd still have to keep those.) Scots often delight in the tale of how, on the day of the passing of the Act of Union in 1707, the bells of St. Giles in Edinburgh had rung out "Why am I so Sad on my Wedding Day". Now we had the answer.

Had we known what we knew now, we may have been played our hand differently. For one thing, we had no idea that one loose remark of the late Alex Salmond's made in the heat of the campaign – that the vote was a "once-in-a-generation opportunity" – would leave us such a hostage to fortune. Even now, many still seem to believe that this phrase was written into the terms of the Edinburgh Agreement itself. We would've been certainly better defended against Project Fear, one of the most shamelessly cynical and anti-democratic operations in British political history. As for "only a vote for No guarantees Scotland a place in Europe" – ten years on, we're not done with the hollow laughter.

Ten years ago – for the first and, we fear, probably the last time in our lives – there was a strong sense that political change was possible in these islands. Those weeks and months were absolutely thrilling. But – and this needs repeating at every opportunity – there were no guns, no bombs, and no violence, nor any threat of it. Crucially, within Scotland there was no "cancelling" of one another. Whether or not anyone else did, in Scotland we let each other speak.

The editors of this volume of essays are both in their early 60s. That means our personal and cultural memories, and our careers as Scottish writers, have unfolded coterminously with the political shift that saw Scottish devolution and independence as a real possibility. We are poets, primarily, and our work is not overtly political in itself. We maintain the absolute right of writers and artists to pursue their own artistic agendas. We are old enough to remember the 1979 devolution referendum (Brexit would have failed too, under the rules imposed on us: 40% of the entire electorate was required to vote "yes"), then the consciousness-raising and nation-building of the 1980s and 90s – with artists and writers boldly at the forefront – which led to the restoration of the Scottish Parliament. We lived through the rise of the SNP under the late Alex Salmond, and the eventual independence referendum of

2014. Most Scottish artists were firmly behind devolution, and "came out" for Scottish independence.

From our teens to our 60s, we have witnessed it all, and we have worked in the hope that our defence of the independence of the artistic mind has made some small contribution to the cultural autonomy Scotland now enjoys – if "enjoys" is currently the right word: we can both recall a time when it was a damn sight more enjoyable, self-confident and classless. But we still do not have political autonomy. So, naturally, that day in our café we asked ourselves: where are we now?

With a view to opening ground on that conversation, we found ourselves both obliged and relieved to accept the kind invitation of an Irish literary magazine to edit an edition devoted to Scotland, a "Stands Scotland Where It Did?" Note: not a Scottish journal; a Belfast-based one. Why? Because no Scottish journal exists which is capable or willing to perform the task. (Rosemary Goring here provides some necessary context on this state of affairs.) Our one remaining long-running, quality literary journal, Gerry Cambridge's *The Dark Horse*, is a poetry-focussed publication, whose funding still has to be sought two issues at a time, even after thirty years of proven excellence.

Having accepted the invitation, our immediate thought was to assemble those writers whose cultural memories were at least as long as our own, or longer. We admit that our programme was partly corrective; recently, the elders have been sidelined. The explanation is, at least in part, a simple one: most of us don't do social media, the medium through which so much cultural business is now conducted. Our defunct print journals were also keepers of memory, tradition, and historical continuity – and radicalism. It has left us, at least in the eyes of the young, looking irrelevant and out-of-touch in a way our own elders did not look to us. The culture wars that further divided us could have been mitigated by intergenerational exchange; we could have traded some valuable life experience in return for some help navigating the greatest sociocultural shift since Gutenberg. Many of the old skills of technique, craft and making have been left to wither and die in the gap between us – skills it was our job to pass on, and the young's responsibility to soak up. But even if we can't tweet for mince, we can still write an essay, so to this more mature group of writers, we issued an invitation. Write something from the perspective of your own area of practice or expertise that concerns Scotland. The essay might consider the state of our politics or civic life, or land use, ecology and climate, or education and universities, or minority languages, or arts, literature and culture and the keeping of the artistic estate. We asked them for essays on Scotland now, and for some speculation, for good or ill, on the decade to come. To those invitations we also added an open call for submissions from any other writers who wished to contribute to the discussion.

This journal is the result. A collection of essays on the keeping of the Scottish cultural estate, discussed in a magazine from across the water which kindly intervened to help us in our hour of need. This issue of *Irish Pages* did receive funding from Creative Scotland, shortly before CS felt compelled to close that funding stream owing to lack of Scottish Government financial commitment. (It has since re-opened, after popular outcry.) The incident drove home the point that while the alliance between Scottish artists and Scottish independence is still a broad one, the perceived allegiance of Scottish artists to the SNP is well and truly over.

So where are we now? In this volume, the elders speak out of that cultural memory. None is happy, none particularly optimistic. The somewhat younger generation included have had to develop their artistic practice and their careers in the digital age; since this represents the principal division between the two generations, they are perhaps better equipped to see, if not more clearly into the future, then differently. To give us a sense of Scotland's youth and vitality, we asked Niall Campbell, himself a fine younger poet, to edit a section of new and emerging poets from Scotland. The poets have forever been the "future dreamers" of the culture, and one ignores their voices at one's peril. This poetry selection rather brings us back full circle. In 1994, Donny O'Rourke published his anthology of New Scottish Poets, *Dream State*. This was published at the peak of the cultural momentum which followed the 1979 referendum, shortly before 74% voted Yes to the Devolution Act of 1997. Both the present editors were included in that volume. We were indeed still in the dream times. The dream seems to have vanished, for now, and in its place is little but empty sleep. But in rest we gather strength. Nonetheless it may be time to wake up and face the reality of Scotland's present situation before we dare dream again.

Kathleen Jamie
Don Paterson

Edinburgh, January 1st, 2025

FOREWORD

Kathleen Jamie is a poet and essayist. Her poetry collections include The Overhaul, *which won the 2012 Costa Poetry Prize, and* The Tree House, *which won the Forward prize.* The Bonniest Company *won the 2015 Saltire Scottish Book of the Year Award. Her non-fiction essays are collected in the three highly regarded books:* Findings, Sightlines, *and* Surfacing, *all regarded as important contributions to the "new nature writing". In 2024 she published* Cairn, *"a view from the strange here-and-now", and* The KeelieHawk, *a collection of poems in Scots.*

Between 2010 and 2020 Kathleen was Professor of Creative Writing at the University of Stirling, and from 2021–24 she served as Scotland's Makar, or National Poet. Kathleen's interests include archaeology, nature and environment, travel and art.

Don Paterson is the author of sixteen books of poetry, aphorism, criticism, memoir and poetic theory. His poetry has won many awards, including the Whitbread Poetry Prize, the Geoffrey Faber Memorial Prize, the Costa Poetry Award, three Forward Prizes, the T.S. Eliot Prize on two occasions, and the Queen's Gold Medal for Poetry. He is a Professor Emeritus at the University of St Andrews and for twenty-five years was Poetry Editor at Picador Macmillan. He has long had a parallel career as a jazz guitarist. He lives in Kirriemuir, Angus.

DEFEATED BUT NEVER CONQUERED?

Neal Ascherson

A mongrel tradition.

Nations wear badges, words usually hung on them lopsidedly by foreigners. Scotland has been unlucky there. "Bonnie" is weakly bearable. "Stern and Wild" now suggests sporting visitors picnicking on a mountainside. "Scotland the Brave"? Once about real soldiers in real wars, it's been defused until it only evokes pipe bands consoling the nation for yet another football defeat snatched from the jaws of victory. Sour syllables. But in the past, there have been better words.

It was in 1628, almost a decade into the Thirty Years War. The Imperial armies were closing on the Baltic port-city of Stralsund, when its desperate citizens sent for the Scots. At the last moment, six companies of Scottish mercenary soldiers and a Swedish battalion slipped into the city and manned its new battlements. With them came Colonel Robert Monro of Foulis, from a clan-family of warriors already fighting for the "Protestant Cause" all over central Europe. His men were to stay there on the wallhead for a solid month, fighting day and night against the ceaseless assaults of the Catholic Emperor's regiments commanded by Wallenstein, the most feared general in Europe. When the enemy at last gave up and withdrew, almost five hundred Scots – more than half of Munro's companions – were dead.

Long afterwards, having survived his own wounds and many more battles, Munro wrote about Stralsund. (No linguist, he called it *Trailesound*). He wondered if the town had been grateful enough, not least to its wartime Scottish governor Sir Alexander Leslie. Something from *Genesis* came to Monro's tough old Calvinist mind. "It faring then with Trailesound as with Sara; she became fruitfull when she could not believe it, and they became flourishing having gotten a Scots Governour to protect them, whom they looked not for, which was a good Omen unto them to get a Governour of the onley Nation, that was never conquered..."

"Never conquered!" That was the badge Robert Monro touched when he considered Scotland. What was the defining boast of France or Bohemia, of England or Saxony – to be the richest or the most God-fearing, to have the most beautiful women or the most fertile soil? Let them choose. For Monro and his generation, it was those seven words about "the onley Nation" which defined Scotland: its badge, its carrying myth. Their country's identity, they believed, lay in its ancient defence of what was called "fredome" – an independent kingdom in which even the "unfree" feudal peasantry need not fear foreign tyranny.

It's true: Scotland was never permanently conquered by the Romans, the Norse or the English. But there were plenty of defeats leading to intervals of occupation. A few years after Stralsund, Oliver Cromwell would deface that badge, invading and crushing the Scots and, in 1652, imposing a short-lived Union which reduced Scotland to little better than an English province. So: "defeated but never conquered"? The doubt points to deeper and darker questions about who we want to be – or to have been. When was Scotland? When will Scotland be?

The "When?" question is a good one. The late Gwyn Alf Williams, socialist and historian agonising for his own Welsh people, set it in the title of his famous book: *When Was Wales?* An essentialist nationalist has an answer: that in a certain dim and distant age, his or her nation was most fully "itself". A better answer is that there are no single defining "Whens". National communities formed themselves, named themselves and changed their shape and habits over the course of millennia studded with lesser "Whens". But Scotland – not only its older historians – has not always avoided the "Big When" fallacy. It has been located in the Wars of Independence, as William Wallace and Robert the Bruce fought the English for "fredome", an Age more heroic than golden. That "When" was proudly accepted for centuries by Scots of high and low degree, even after the 1707 Union. More recently, though, the eighteenth-century Scottish Enlightenment has been marketed as Scotland's "When". Glorious intellectual effulgence, certainly. But experienced only by a smallish elite whose radiance scarcely touched the common mass living in the shadows of hunger, poverty and the fear of eviction.

Apart from such "Whens", Scots have not bothered to picture their nation as some Hegelian self-realising subject, a unity moving up its escalator of destiny. They have good reasons for that. Far from being "unconquered", Scotland slowly emerged from a scramble of petty conquests and conflicts: Picts, Dalriadic Gaels, Norse raiders and settlers, Anglian invaders, "British" Celtic-speakers in Strathclyde and the Lothians. This jostling assembly gradually – in ways still not well understood – was unified under Dalriadic rulers whose Gaelic language became for a time general. Scribes began to write about a "Scottish people" long before their kingdom of Alba became known as Scotland.

These beginnings explain why, in contrast to so many other small nationalities, Scots don't pose as an "ethnicity". That great European, Hubert Butler of Kilkenny, once wrote about a conference seeking to soothe the Troubles that "the Forum failed… but left a lingering sweetness in the air. The desire for unity and harmony is something like the desire to sleep."

It's true that late-mediaeval writers followed the European fashion for inventing unifying lineages: the 1320 Declaration of Arbroath proclaimed the Scots to be a noble immigrant tribe from Greater Scythia. But that fable – implying "racial" homogeneity – perished under Enlightenment scorn. Every schoolchild today is supposed to know that Scotland began in diversity: a society made by immigrants speaking anything from Irish or Norse to Punjabi or Polish. This is why, many years ago, the novelist Willie McIlvanney raised such a tremendous cheer when he told a nationalist rally in Edinburgh that "Scottishness is not some pedigree lineage. This is a mongrel tradition!"

This inclination to accept solid difference rather than fuzzy unity applies also to land and people. In Scotland, the two keep their distance. In southern England, people often talk affectionately of the green fields and thyme-scented downlands as "English", as if they were an estate inseparable from its owners. In Scotland, geology and history leave the human population and the landscape wary of one another. Asking reader's tolerance, I repeat what I have written elsewhere about this stony realm where the soil is often thin and acid, and where, seen in long perspective, "human settlement and activity are no more than a form of lichen which can take hold in the least exposed crevices and surfaces of the land… the rock pokes through the worn sleeve of the turf." It's significant how often children in Scotland – especially those brought up in steep cities – struggle to make a distinction between the living rock of cliff and outcrop and the massive blocks of castle walls or bridges. When they do grow old enough to recognise the illusion for what it is, that wariness between human and landscape sets in. And yet Scotland's literary imagination plays incurably with its childrens' wide-eyed vision. I mean the terrifying suspicion that, after all, the gap between life and non-life may not be absolute. Why is it that the words "Living Stone" retain such magnetism in this country – the name of a town, of a religious community set among megaliths, of a lonely and unsuccessful missionary who became Scotland's lay saint?

In his poem "On A Raised Beach", Hugh MacDiarmid honoured stones as invulnerable in their essence – "There are plenty of ruined buildings in the world but no ruined stones." And yet he also recognised them as "sensitive in their own way" to "This cat's cradle of life, this reality volatile yet determined; / This intense vibration in the stones / That makes them seem immobile to us..." Modern archaeology assigns a biography to everything, human artefact or environmental splinter, to the bog body, the bronze axe-head laid beside it and the slow-spreading peat blanket which covers them both. The late Stanley Eveling took this point about life in the unliving. An Edinburgh playwright and philosopher, he worked in the city which crouches before the gigantic geology lesson of Salisbury Craigs, and he wrote: "An object is a slow event."

Scotland's neolithic first-farmers wanted faster events, which they could eat. They accelerated objects. They cleared the stony débris left by the glaciations and pierced the soil with digging-sticks, then foot-ploughs. They shared out land use, the rough out-by and hill for the collective's pasture, arable rigs for crops and individuals. It's hard now to imagine that up to about 1750, when the Lowland and then the Highland Clearance began to uproot whole populations, almost every living person in Scotland had some sort of written or (usually) unwritten title to land. The scale of it varied from the wide acres of a laird to the patch of acid earth allotted for the use of a cottar family in a Highland joint-tenancy. If that sounds idyllic, of course it was not. Folk on the land lived in danger of crop failure and famine, of passing war-gangs and the predation of feudal superiors. But, remarkably, something of that sense of a natural right to the land has survived. It held on even after agricultural "improvement" had cleared away the old "ferm touns" and Highland joint settlements, privatised the "commonties" and driven their people to the cities or the emigrant ships.

In this century, devolved Scottish governments – through tentative land reforms and the encouragement of "community buy-outs" – have so far shared this assumption that a hill, a fertile strath, a loch can never quite be "private property" in the absolute English sense. Most Scots, I think, assume that we are lawfully entitled to tread where we please in our own country (always respecting lambing-time and anxious cows with young followers). But that legal assumption is heavily qualified in practice. In a countryside dominated – its uplands especially – by a handful of vast private estates, the "right to roam" needs constantly fought for.

Urbanization, the migration from country to towns and cities, happened more rapidly in Scotland than anywhere else in Europe – including England. In 1750, 9.2 per cent of Scots lived in towns with over 10,000 inhabitants. By

1850, that figure had exploded to 32 per cent, reaching 60 per cent in 1911 (latterly, almost all of it into big town with populations of over 50,000). The push was agricultural improvement. The pull was massive and breakneck industrialisation, starting with textiles and ending the century with world-renowned production of coal and steel, ships, locomotives and spectacular feats of civil engineering.

One lasting outcome of this speed of change was its impact on public health, collapsing in slum squalor. Sir Tom Devine writes in his history *The Scottish Nation: 1700 to 2000* that "if the standard of 'overcrowding'… of more than two persons to a room had been applied to Scotland in 1918, 45 per cent of the population, or a remarkable total of over 2 million people, were living in overcrowded conditions." Made worse by the poverty and wage insecurity of this new proletariat, by lack of sunlight and wretched diet, health became an enduring crisis of lethal epidemics, infant mortality, and sheer physical stunting. (Looking back in shame, how could my young self have taken it as just "a Glasgow thing" that every pub held a "wee man" whose chin scarcely reached the bar?) Even now after so much has changed for the better, there remain in Scotland intractable patches of terrible health (inaccurately called "the Glasgow Effect") where heart disease and liver failure are rampant and where life expectancy is a decade shorter than in "better" streets less than a mile away. Is it possible we have a case of "epigenetics" – the half-understood transmission of environmental health damage from one generation to its children and even further? The Dutch grandchildren of those damaged as infants by the Nazi starvation-punishment in 1945 now often evince the same cluster of heart, hepatic and obesity symptoms. It's been suggested that ill health in the Caribbean today relates to the multiple impacts of slavery and post-slavery servitude. Might not the puzzling bad health in parts of Scotland, persistent even after the mid-twentieth century brought the National Health Service and radical re-housing, be an inheritance from those early deprivations?

Another outcome of the great uprooting was an enduring fear of betrayal. Societies based on traditional loyalties – service in return for protection – fell apart. Gaelic chieftains had evicted their own clansmen and replaced them with sheep. Lowland lairds exchanged tenants for turnips and new-fangled farming methods. Here and there in the Highlands and islands there was real resistance and violence, eventually persuading London to pass the Crofting Acts of the 1880s. And yet Scotland never saw the huge and bloody peasant risings which challenged landowning classes all over Europe in the same nineteenth century, opening the way – generations later – to the establishment of free landowning peasantries on their own fields. Neither were there "Land Wars" in Scotland to compare with the huge scale, ferocity and persistence of land rebellions in Ireland. Scotland seethed with radical ideas during and after the French Revolution, provoking merciless judicial terror. The 1820 "Radical War", a workers' conspiracy for "liberty" and democratic rights, brought all Glasgow out on strike but dissolved when an armed splinter group was defeated by government cavalry.

In 1848, stateless nationalities all over Europe went to the barricades for liberty and national independence. But in Scotland the land lay still. "Scotland the Brave" cheered foreign rebellions against despotism, but avoided criticising its own Union with England – just as the 1820 revolutionaries had not called for independence but for a simultaneous rising by English workers. After the Radical War, Lord Cockburn jested that Edinburgh had been "quiet as the grave, or as Peebles". The "nation that was never conquered", and certainly never colonised like Ireland, seemed to have colonised itself.

The "unconquered" myth was now domesticated into the cult of "the Scottish Soldier". In his book *Empireworld* (2023) Sathnam Sanghera remarks on how the British identified and enlisted "martial races" in the Empire (Hausa, Gurkha, Punjabi…) and trained them to parade with versions of their "native" war-clothing, weaponry and music. And the first "martial race" to be enlisted, in the eighteenth century, was the Scottish Highlanders. Soon proverbial for courage and ferocity, Scottish (not only Highland) regiments would patrol the Empire and suffer terrible, disproportionate losses in two World Wars. Pride in them – and in their banner-loyalty to the Empire – was intense. Indeed, it's been argued that by stoking the furnace of "loyal" Scottish militarism, the Tory-Unionist party represented popular patriotism far more authentically, up to about 1950, than the still-marginal SNP. The capture of Quebec, the relief of Lucknow, the sacrifice on the Somme, hunting down Mau Mau in Kenya and finally ("the last battle of the British Empire") the 1967 storm of the Aden Crater by Mad Mitch and the 1st Argylls, were all clasps on a medal soon to be stowed away in a drawer.

Scotland only began to "decolonise" itself in the mid-twentieth century. This partly took the form of political nationalism, driven by increasing disillusion with Scotland's subordination in the United Kingdom. But another source of change was moral and historical: a series of painful self-discoveries. In the British Empire, the "never conquered nation" had helped vigorously to conquer and humiliate other nationalities. A feeble version of "we were only obeying orders" was in circulation, implying that imperial atrocities and exploitations were essentially English. This amnesia dishonoured public memory for decades. Meanwhile, "down south", English and Caribbean historians set about revising conventional stories of Empire. It was London scholars who published the 1834 compensation lists for abolition, revealing the enormous extent of Scottish ownership and management of Caribbean slave plantations – not to mention Glasgow's enthusiastic investment in Atlantic slave-ships. More would emerge and reach an initially resentful public: the Scottish share in the plundering of India, the massacre of aboriginal populations in Australia by Gaelic settlers who were themselves victims of the Clearances. Such revelations continue. But after the centuries of hypocrisy, they are acting as a liberating wind from the sea. Scottish politics may now be heading into a stagnant season. But Scots suddenly hold more knowledge about one another than was permitted to their fathers. In a nation whose writers, artists and other intellectuals are today almost without exception the children of working-class parents, this breakthrough in history is also a class barrier falling.

The "matter of Scotland", the question of independence, has been the underlying debate in the nation for some fifty years now. The grip of independence on half the country's imaginations – the poorer, more precarious half – seems immovable, almost immune to the fluctuating fortunes of a nationalist party. The percentage of those who see themselves as "Scottish only" slowly grows; the "Scottish and British" identity is dissolving more rapidly. And in the debate, the deadliest word has been "normal", as in: "I just want Scotland to be a normal wee nation like the others."

Normal wee nations talk to one another, borrow from one another. Scotland, which voted so powerfully and vainly in 2016 to remain in the European Union, once imported culture from France and the Netherlands as much as from England. In the twentieth century, ranging Scots brought home Expressionism from Germany, architecture and *Jugendstyl* decoration from Vienna, film culture from Hungary, Poland and France. Now the disaster of Brexit is turning into a process, as Westminster politicians go round closing one British window on the outside world after another and drawing the curtains. Scotland, so specially dependent on Polish or Lithuanian immigration, on Scandinavian ideas for social care, on German models for truly responsible local government, on visas for European theatres and orchestras, is beginning to find it hard to breathe. The growing economic damage is blatant, confessed even at Westminster. A time is approaching when the United Kingdom will be a suffocating place that young people want to leave. Scotland may have reconquered and decolonised itself, may even have reached a new degree of moral independence. But to perish "unconquered" and asphyxiated by a suicidal neighbour is no sort of victory.

One of Scotland's most revered writers, Neal Ascherson was born in Edinburgh in 1932. His books include The King Incorporated Leopold II *(Allen & Unwin, 1963);* Games with Shadows *(Radius, 1989);* The Polish August; The Struggles for Poland; Black Sea; Stone Voices *(Granta); and* The Death of the Fronsac *(Head of Zeus, 2017). He was the central and eastern Europe correspondent for* The Observer *for many years. He also covered southern and central Africa for* The Observer *and* The Scotsman *from 1969–1989 and was the Scottish politics correspondent for* The Scotsman *from 1975–1979. From 1998 until 2008, he was Editor of* Public Archaeology, *a journal from the Institute of Archaeology at UCL, as well as a columnist for* The Observer *and* Independent on Sunday *1985–2008. He lives in London and Argyll.*

AT ACHNABREAC

Dougie Strang

A cup's sip.

On a damp evening, a year after moving to Argyll, I visited the prehistoric rock art at Achnabreac. I'd been reading archaeological studies of the site, as well as interpretations of what the art might mean – fascinating, insightful work – but my head was full and I wanted to encounter the art just as it was, be present to it. I was also curious to explore how it might relate, if at all, to the work of artists today. The fact that it was just down the road, and that I could drop by on an impulse, was still novel to me.

Achnabreac is an exposed outcrop of rock that protrudes from the surrounding land like a humped back, splitting the turf at the seams. Twenty thousand years ago, the Devensian Ice Sheet was the last of many glaciers to scour its surface smooth, making it a useful canvas for art. The outcrop hosts the largest accumulation of prehistoric rock carvings in the British Isles. It's part of what has come to be called the ritual landscape of Kilmartin Glen – a glen that brims with archaic culture; with hill forts and standing stones, chambered cairns and rock art panels. The carvings at Achnabreac are typical of those found in Argyll and elsewhere in Scotland, and share features with carvings found in a few concentrated locations in England and Wales, Ireland, Brittany in France, and in North-West Spain and Portugal.

There were no cars in the carpark and the track I followed was gloomy, overshadowed on one side by plantation forestry. A steady breeze just about kept the midges at bay. When I reached the site, I hopped the stile over the railing and climbed onto the upper half of the outcrop. The rock beneath my feet was glazed by the day's rain, highlighting the carvings. I took care not to step on them. I say "carvings", but "peckings" would be more appropriate, the art created through repeated hammering, or pecking, with a quartz axe, each blow dislodging small flakes of stone. It's a technique that was first used at Achnabreac around five thousand years ago, with subsequent carvings made from the Late Neolithic through to the Early Bronze Age – a span of at least a thousand years.

"Here we are," the carvings say, still holding the presence of those who carved them. You can see individual peck marks, like the brush or knife strokes visible in impasto painting, and so more easily imagine the axe and the hand that held it, the fingers ingrained with rock dust. Whatever motivated the carvers, whatever their purpose in creating this art, is lost to us; all we know is that they committed to the task, leaning in to the surface of the outcrop as I was now.

The carvings were made before Scotland had a notion of itself, before even the concept of nation states; and I don't think it's necessary to understand their meaning – I don't think you need a theory of Neolithic Cosmology – in order to recognise that their longevity gives them cohesion and confidence; the kind that comes from a thousand years of practice, honed by generations, from an enduring commitment to place, culture and community. This is what draws me to Achnabreac: a sense that the art here is testament to a way of being that was sustained and celebrated for millennia; that thrived within the ecological limits of this coastal region we now call Argyll, living off what resources the land and sea provided, finding rapport with the more-than-human world.

The art at Achnabreac is not complex, limited as it is to a series of repeated, abstract motifs: shallow cups pecked into the surface of the rock, often surrounded by concentric rings that are broken by a single groove radiating from the centre. But as with any art, there's purpose in the placing. Some cups and rings are clustered together, deliberately adjacent to one another, while others are placed in relation to cracks in the rock, so that the carving is framed by or in some cases penetrated by the cracks; and while there's no sense of the carvings being arranged to present a harmonious whole, the accumulative effect is impressive: the outcrop teems with art, hums with it, is animated by it.

The Romanian scholar of myth and ritual, Mircea Eliade, called such places hierophanies, from the Greek *hieros*, sacred, and *pháneia*, to reveal. A hierophany, then, is an object or place that is seen to manifest the sacred, whether it's as simple as a carved wooden cross or as complex as a river system. These are not symbols. The outcrop at Achnabreac is not symbolically sacred; it is sacred. At least, it is to those comfortable with the idea that places hold and express a preternatural or otherworldly essence, one that exists beyond material reality.

Elsewhere, Achnabreac might be given over to the stewardship of cultural elders, who would ensure that those who visit the site do so with a respectful awareness of its significance. Here in Scotland, we put up railings and interpretation panels. The panels speculate meaning and function, acknowledging only that the origins of the art *might* lie in sacred practice, and if so, it's a practice that is firmly consigned to the past.

But what does it say to the present; what kind of mirror, if any, does it hold? As well as endurance, cohesion and confidence, as well as a reminder of a way of being that was ecologically balanced, the art at Achnabreac demonstrates that Argyll was once part of an arc of culture that stretched over a thousand miles from here to Portugal. We know little about that culture, whether in Argyll or Cork, Brittany or Galicia, but the art forms that it shared, the carved cups and rings, suggests that at least some of its customs and beliefs were held in common. Significant too is that all of these places were, and still are, connected by an Atlantic seaboard that, as the poet Kenneth White has it, "governs our territory, creating the weather, shaping the coasts, wavelengthing minds."

Back in 2007, I attended NVA's performance, *Half Life*, here in the forest at Achnabreac. At the time, NVA was one of the most ambitious arts organisations in Scotland – the name is an acronym of *nacionale vita activa*, from the Ancient Greek ideal of a lively democracy. NVA was renowned for its large-scale outdoor installations and performances, most famously at the Old Man of Storr on Skye; but in the end, it couldn't secure funding to match its ambition. The attempt to turn St Peter's Seminary, a modernist ruin near Cardross in Argyll, into a centre for public art and debate was its undoing, and the organisation closed in 2018.

Perhaps NVA's closure was inevitable in straitened times, with arts funding, along with so many other services, pared back to the bone; but I miss it, I miss its confidence, I miss what it had to say to Scotland and to the world.

The evening performance of *Half Life* in the forest was accompanied by a series of installations that could be visited during the day at sites throughout Kilmartin Glen – including work by Japanese sound artist, Toshiya Tsunoda. The experience was, for me, a rare and powerful encounter with art and theatre as ritual. What's more, it engaged with Scotland's heritage in a way that was neither nostalgic nor parochial. It seemed to align, instead, with White's vision of an Atlantic culture – one that is shaped by our relationship to a specific landscape, but which is also expansive, outward looking, hospitable to what the sea might bring to its shores.

If we allow that the cups and rings at Achnabreac have meaning beyond being simply decorative, then by carving them into the outcrop, the carvers have released that meaning from the constraint of time. Thousands of years later, it's still here, still held in the rock, still puzzling us; and I'm glad that the interpretation panels on the site are kept to a minimum, glad that on a damp evening you can find yourself alone with the art – like being let loose in a museum after closing-time – with space and time to reach towards your own relationship with it.

The cups had gathered water from the day's rain. I knelt down and tried to drink the water from one of them, though I'm not sure why. Its small size and lack of a lip, the fact that it couldn't be tipped, made it difficult, but I persevered, pressed my face against the rock, managed a couple of awkward sips.

I'm wary of words like "hierophany", "preternatural", "otherworldly"; wary of the mystical fug that often accumulates around sites like Achnabreac. The hard fact is that it's just a lump of rock with some old carvings on it. Yet I'm drawn again and again to such places, and to experiences that pull me towards the metaphysical territory they inhabit. Perhaps, despite my ingrained Presbyterian scepticism, I'm drawn because I recognise that the alternative is not serving us well – a society that abjures any kind of "sacred practice", considering it to be unnecessary, redundant.

This year, in Kilmartin Glen, local artist Susannah Rose organised a lantern walk along the banks of the River Add, to welcome the spring salmon back to the river. A respectful borrowing from traditions outwith Scotland, this was art and performance as a means to deepen the community's relationship with the wildlife of the glen – in this case, some of the few salmon that still manage to return to its rivers.

I think it's useful to keep asking what art is for, and what kind of art we most need in this century of climate and ecological crisis. For all that I miss the confidence and ambition of NVA, I'm not sure that this is a time for large-scale, spectacular productions. Perhaps it's more appropriate to support artists, whether urban or rural, who work on a more modest scale, and who take their communities with them as participants rather than spectators. Perhaps we need art that creates patterns of meaning and ceremony, that reaffirms the connection between people and place, culture and nature.

On the outcrop at Achnabreac, after focusing so intently on the carvings, I was surprised when I stood up and found that the night had settled around me. The sky was clouded and there was no moon or stars. A few miles to the south, I could see the lights of Lochgilphead, clustered around the head of the sea loch. I walked down to the carpark through the hush of the forest. Trees loomed at me in the dark and my feet drummed on the path as though the ground beneath was hollow. In the car, lights on, engine running, I was bemused by myself: sipping from a Neolithic cup, as if it had been pecked for that purpose; as if, in drinking from it, I was taking communion with those who'd made it.

Dougie Strang was born in Glasgow in 1966. He has an MA Hons in Scottish Ethnology from University of Edinburgh. He is the author of The Bone Cave: A Journey Through Myth and Memory *(Birlinn, 2023) and a contributor to* Antlers of Water: Writing on the Nature and Environment of Scotland *(Canongate, 2020, edited by Kathleen Jamie). He is a regular contributor to* Dark Mountain *and to online the journal* Bella Caledonia. *He is currently researching and writing a book about belonging and exile. He lives in Argyll.*

TWO MINUTES' PANDEMONIUM

Colin Bramwell

Cat's een.

Scots is the maist widely-kent minority leid in the UK: accordin tae the lest census, we've 1.5 milyin speakers, and jist aboot twa milyin kenners. ("And that's jist in Scotland, mate!" – said The Ass.) In private, maist Scottish poets huv haed thir misgivins oan the veracity ae thon feegur. An owerestimation – hou mony ae thaim's actually spikkin filly Scots day-tae-day? An unnerestimation – as Scots hus a 98% similarity wae English (for reference tweesh Spanish and Portuguese it's ninety) whit's gaein oan wae thae three million wha say they dinna ken a single ward, seein as hou they cannae *aa* be Rangers fans? Bit that's the Scots fur ye: whaur extremes meet.

Fur the uninitiatit, Scots is the tongue ablo wir tongue. The leid is like a shilpie, hauf-eaten conjyned twin ae English. In fact, the language comes fae England, and used tae be cried "Inglis" an aa. Written Scots hus baith heich "literary" and low "demotic" registers. Jist like English, Scots literature's scrieved at present in a balance ae baith registers at wance; jist like English, the heich register ae Scots is mair challengin inwae the owerall English context whaur thon wark's aye read. Soonds different – reads differenter – and yet, wance yir in the flow ae it, it's no sae haurd tae ken.

That being said, reader, nice one for making it even this far. We'll switch between English and Scots from now on, just to sugar the horse pill I'm asking you to swallow here. Sorry, but it might well constitute a cure. If it helps, the present author is a doctor – just not of the useful variety – however, after studying Scots for a number of years he has come to believe that this language does have a medicinal purpose for English. Scots, and other languages like it, redress the singularity of English, refreshing it, keeping it fertile through contact with other tongues. Though English dominates Scots, perhaps it will never do so entirely, because the success of English has had the effect of prolonging the life of Scots – while simultaneously depleting it. By now poets in Scotland have figured out that this linguistic situation of ours is as comic as it is tragic. In the very act of mourning Scots, we always seem to pull it from the grave. However, although linguistic health is a byproduct of writers' activities, this cannot be our main/only goal. To repurpose the Boromir meme, one does not simply write in Scots. In other words, a crap poem in any language is still a crap poem. Gott sei Dank.

———

"Poetry is political!"– the dullard's cry. Obviously this is different to saying that poetry is politics and politics alone, though one suspects that's what the Twitterati mean these days. One thinks of Yeats's interest in the occult: he said this enabled him "to hold in a single thought reality and justice". Are Scots poets paying sufficient attention to the former? Hugh MacDiarmid, for example, struggled to balance these: latterly he seemed more concerned with reality than justice. But at present it seems that our deep desire for justice threatens to drag us further from reality. Either way, classic self-defeat.

———

Wan decade syne wir last self-defeatin referendum, we're close tae hae the centenary ae MacDiarmid's masterpiece, *A Drunk Man Looks at the Thistle*. Oan the man's daith, Norman MacCaig said they shid observe twa minutes' pandemonium. Fine description ae MacDiarmid himself, as much as whit he unleashed. MacDiarmid wiss Scotland's ultimate political poet. We winna rehearse the man's mony faults here – "problematic", says Heaney. Aye. And in spite ae this, MacDiarmid's mair important tae the cause ae Scots and Scotland than ony ither poet fae the previous century. "My job, as I see it, has never been to lay a tit's egg, but to erupt like a volcano, emitting not only flame, but a lot of rubbish." And that's hou Mount MacDiarmid maun be regarded: tempted as we micht be tae tak oot the rubbish, we canna thraw the hail lot awa, as wull shairly be settin the bins ablaze. And whit's mair self-defeatin nor a bin fire?

———

MacDiarmid eventually switched to English because, in his own words, he wanted "a poetry of fact and first-hand experience and scientific knowledge that is right about every technical detail." It is this switch in mission of MacDiarmid's – a desire to subordinate poetry to a different pole of intellectual discourse – that explains why his later English stuff, though some of it is excellent, never quite reaches the heights of the earlier work in Scots. In late MacDiarmid, the reader and writer are confronted with such an overwhelming vision of scientific reality that both may be likely to lose sight of justice. MacDiarmid at – not his worst – let's say most dull – exemplifies the opposite of Keats's negative capability: "of being in uncertainties, Mysteries, doubts, without any irritable reaching after fact and reason". I reckon if Keats was Scottish, he would have just said *in vino veritas*. In *A Drunk Man*, early MacDiarmid animates the spirit of one pisshead who comes to stand for all of humanity, and the negatively capable speaker of that poem clears the route, not to science, but to the other side of the coin – a mature humanism expressed through blethers. Joyce's territory.

Governance? Wull, Northern-Irish reader, I haurdly need tae bitch tae yirsels aboot Westminster, Tories, Brexit: aa's tae be said oan that is, they seem tae gie even less ae a shit aboot yous than they do aboot us. Houiver, as whingein tae Irish people about hou crap Scotland is is a noble tradition here – wan wir uphaudin in thon issue ae yir *Pages* – lat's dae it.

Now I'm going to risk alienating my entire readership by suggesting that Scotland at present might have something to learn from England – or perhaps, more accurately, from an ironic joyful element in English popular culture. Perhaps you'll have already seen this thing that Spurs fans do sometimes, when they're losing. They all start chanting "Let's pretend we've scored a goal", then launch into celebrations. Well, I'm going to suggest that this is pretty much the right model for thinking about how to bring an independent Scotland into being. Strengthening languages and arts would be a necessary first step in the creation of an independent Scotland. Why not do this now? Why not just go ahead and act like we're scoring this goal – and in so doing actually score it? Within that pretense, a nation's culture may be found. As Scottish artists we are used to hearing Alasdair Gray's dictum: work as though you live in the early days of a better nation. This is what all artists here, everywhere, do. Time for politicians in Scotland to start heeding Gray, to start taking culture seriously here – and to stop running arts on a shoestring. If the Scottish Poetry Library, for instance, is (according to our government's present fierce-mild "Scots policy") meant to be a crucial "stakeholder" in Holyrood's strategy for Scots, how come its grant is less than half the size of Poetry Ireland's? (Note: My calculation here is drawn from looking at the accounts of both Poetry Ireland and the Scottish Poetry Library in the comparatively financially-sunny uplands of 2020. PI, by the way, run Ireland's flagship magazine, *Poetry Ireland Review*. But reader, perhaps you've heard of Scotland's equivalent? It's called *Irish Pages*.)

The argument that the SNP post-Brexit have been too focused on independence is right enough, and has been proven by the party's embarrassing mismanagement of funds that were intended to go towards campaigning for a second referendum. Again, if you don't know this story, Google "SNP campervan" for the second-most egregious example of self-defeat in recent Scottish history. (Then, for the most egregious, Google "Humza Yousaf downfall".) Even through the boke-inducing trial of Alex Salmond, his successor seemed to run a pretty steady ship. Nicola Sturgeon was the most capable politician in Britain for a time. Fatally, though, under her watch the SNP failed to realise that effective devolved government will make a far better case for future independence than mere agitation in the courts. We have great problems in Scotland that must be addressed now. The civic issue of Scottish languages, for instance, cannot wait for independence. Scottish Gaelic has been predicted by experts to die out within my own generation. We cannot thole this. If a nationalist government continue to preside over the demise of Gaelic, they will have no right to act as though they are the mouthpiece for the Scottish people – no right to call themselves nationalists. And the same will be true if the question of Scots remains insubstantially addressed by Holyrood here.

Noo, lat's be fair. Syne the SNP tuik the reins, they huvnae dune nothin. Neist tae nothin? Aye, unfair. It wid be a gey intristin thocht experiment tae chart hou the awaukenin ae national consciousness aroon the referendum micht hae fed intae my ain generation ae Scottish poets' seemin-comfort scrievin in the leid. It wiss a guid thing fur us here, the referendum. A fairer fecht nor Brexit. Fur a time it seemed like a better future fur Scotland wiss possible. Some torpor's tae be expectit eftir sic disappointments – bit, as ony Drunk Man wid tell ye, the world disappoints. Onyweys, Scots can noo be studied fae S3–S6 level; the leid's discussed anaa in anither course, Scottish Studies. Nane's compulsory. It's still possible tae gae throu schuil in Scotland and anely encoonter the Scots leid in the wark ae Burns, in poetry. Thon's a sign ae wir poetry's strenth; and, widdershins, tells ye that wir no takkin the leid seriously aneuch tae liberate it fae verse.

In Wales the study ae Welsh is compulsory fae the stert ae yir education tae the age ae 16. And we've gat twice the amoont ae fowk here aye claim tae spikk Scots. Whit a chance is bein missed. If English is yir erst leid and ye live in Scotland, Scots wull be the easiest ither tongue fur ye tae learn. Houiver, as ithers huv observed, Burns is aye bein asked tae dae some pretty heavy liftin the noo. We need a proper strategy oan Scots education: if we want wir leid tae continue, we need tae mak it compulsory in schuils, fae day wan. Excludin Gaelic-speakin territories, thirs pretty much nae pairt ae Scotland whaur Scots isnae spoken. The fact that we huvna thocht tae folla the Welsh example here shaas wir government hus a dearth ae ambition oan the issue ae wir leids. Seems like we cannae even follae wir *ain* example oan Gaelic – Gaelic-language schuils in Scotland are thrivin the noo. The alternative tae makin thae types ae interventions in education is tae condemn wir leid tae the status ae a curio tongue. Scots maun be taught like ony ither language: but erst, it maun be taught.

Giein the abune, micht we declare a moratorium oan SNP airse-kissin fae Scottish poets – jist till the abune is sorted? Personally I've foond it caller tae hae a makar whas kept thir distance. The makar is fur the people, nae fur the party – jist in case onywan needs remindin.

Richt, accordin tae the Balmoral clock thit rins three minutes fast ootside Waverley Station – jist sae fowk are oan time fur thir trains – I've gat forty seconds left here tae complete my point. Aneuch whingein. I wantit tae mention twa alumni fae Belfast's Heaney Centre. I mean twa mair doctors ae the useless variety: Scott McKendry an Charles Lang. McKendry first, whas debut *Gub* conteens a footnote section that seems tae constitute a bittie mair nor a third ae the book itsel. In thon we learn that "gab"s the Scottish wey tae say the mair Belfasty "gub". That's bollocks. Bollocks, houiver, is a solid generic choice fur McKendry. Acc tae see Ulsterese been drawn oan sic a wey; an authentic thread ae unremittin gobshite animatin the wark. The Belfast tradition's bein cared fur weel here; excited tae see whit McKendry does wae it.

Charles Lang hails fae Glesca. We've hud a swatch ae his erst full buik, *The Oasis*, oot wae Dublin's ain Skein Press neist year. Tae extend MacCaig's pandemonium metafur: in the *Paradise Lost* ae present-day Scots poetry, Charles Lang may someday be wir Gabriel. Thirs an angelic quality tae the wark; gallus like Leonard, bit kinder, mair personable, mair experimental inwae the lyric airt. In Lang's leid, yud be haurd-pressed tae tell whit's tweesh Scots and English. Fur the praisent author, thon fact maun pit him oan the side ae the vernacular angels wha even nou keep poetry true on its coorse: relevance fur the nonspecialist reader, wha likely speaks the twa at aince. Same fur McKendry. Christ bit we need mair ae *thae* poets the noo.

Given the shared linguistic heirship tweesh territories and traditions, fur the sake ae poetics alane Scotland and Northern Ireland shud muive taewarts establishin thir ain union. Mair veneration ae saintly figures wid be guid fur us – celebratin Edwin Morgan's fine, deserved, bit ye fear he's the anely wan ae thon generation whas bein read in proper detail bi the yoof here. A bit mair Scottish isolation/individuation fae equivalent figures in NI poetry micht pay dividends fur Belfast's praisant young team an aa: in spite ae some terrific wark, thirs a sense ae shadows needin tae be stepped ootae. That said, gin thirs a bit mair cohesion in whit's happenin poetically in Northern Ireland the noo, some credit maun be takken bi the aforementioned Heaney Centre, an institution that gaithers aa the inheritors ae a specific poetical tradition unner the wan ruif – the ruif ae the Woodworkers Pub – an maks them aa get pished thegither. *In vino veritas.*

Sure, thirs comparable programmes in Scotland, bit at praisent seein a Scottish student oan, say, an Edinburgh University Creative Writing masters, wull be like deekin oot a unicorn in the wild fur maist ae that same programme's American attendees. Ye dinnae *need* university tae be a poet, bit thirs aye a reason hou come sae mony ae the Edwin Morgan Poetry Award winners/shortlistees haud, or wull haud, thae degrees. It's mentorin, commonweal, time tae read and tae scrieve; aa useful fur the apprenticeship. Scots wha graduate fae thae institutions dae, sometimes, scrieve in Scots leid an aa. Houiver thae Scots'll tend tae be as middle-class as the majority ae the foreign students. At praisent, wae fundin dreein up in baith the humanities and arts, we maun pynt oot thirs a major access issue here, wan that wull affect warkin-class Scottish students mair, seein as hou thon demographic's mair likely to speak and scrieve in Scots. Bit somehou even eftir bleedin a decent section ae the American an Chinese middle-classes dry, wir universities say thir aye strapped, and the blame game conteenas tweesh thaim, Holyrood and Westminster. *Wull*, as an angry Scottish mither on YouTube wance said, *it was fuckin wanayiz*. Meanwhile, subsequent generations ae Scottish poets wait patiently fur wir ain standard-bearers tae hurry up an win the Nobel Prize, cus aiblins thon's whit it'll tak fur wir ain young poets tae gat the tent that Northern Ireland's huv the noo.

O I ha'e Silence left – an jist as weel, seein as hou accordin tae the clock wir train's in Livingston bi noo. Ach, but wull tyne ye wae some apostasy fae wir ain century-auld Lucifer. Heaney – St Michael? – said MacDiarmid "sacrificed himself to an envisaged standard." Thon standard, gin we'd like tae name it, wiss synthesis tweesh humanist-poetical an nationalist-political spheres. Thon standard that hus led tae an advanced, higher Scots tradition in wir poetry. Noo the neist stage wull be fur poets tae demand the existence ae Advanced Higher Scots in the educational sphere an aa. A political demand: bit no jist political. We maun learn wir leids in Scotland, or tyne them furaye. Paltry tae say the loss ae Scots wid be bad fur Scottish poetry alane, whun it's wir hail culture that's at stake here.

Bit thirs aye licht in the daurk, and the tradition ae Scots poetry proves that the wey furrit is throu. Blake said Milton wiss ae the Devil's pairty withoot kennin it. MacDiarmid at his best wiss aye oan God's – and oan Heaney's an aa.

"Let there be Licht," said God, and there was
A little: but He lacked the poo'er
To licht up mair than pairt o' space at aince,
And there is lots o' darkness that's the same
As gin He'd never spoken
— Mair darkness than there's licht,
And dwarfin' tae a candle-flame,
A spalin' candle that'll sune gang oot.
— Darkness comes closer to us than the licht,
And is oor natural element. We peer oot frae't
Like cat's een bleezin' in a goustrous nicht
(Whaur there is nocht to find but stars
That look like ither cats' een),
Like cat's een, and there is nocht to find
Savin' we turn them in upon oorsels;
Cats canna.

From *A Drunk Man Looks at the Thistle*

Colin Bramwell was born in Irvine, Ayrshire, but grew up further north in Scotland, on the Black Isle. His first degree was in English literature, from University of Edinburgh, with a year abroad at McGill University. His masters degree was in eighteenth-century English Literature, from the University of Oxford. His doctorate at the University of St Andrews was in Creative Writing; for this, he wrote on the methods and meanings of translating poetry into Scots in the present-day. His publications include The Highland Citizenship Test *(Stewed Rhubarb, 2021),* Decapitated Poetry *(co-translations of Taiwanese poet Ko-hua Chen, Seagull Books, 2023), and* beyond *(edited collection of Aonghas Macneacail's later English-language poetry, Shearsman, 2024). His book of Scots translations of Fernando Pessoa,* Fower Pessoas, *will be coming out in early 2025 with Carcanet. He won the 2018 John Dryden Translation Competition for his translations of the Taiwanese poet Yang Mu.* Decapitated Poetry *received the Lucien Stryk Asian Translation Prize, the most prestigious award of its kind in the US. He now lives in Edinburgh with his partner Eva Paredes and their son Pablo.*

TRUTH-WINDOW

Kate Molleson

Blink and you miss it.

In the summer of 1945, the Hungarian composer Béla Bartók was in exile in New York City. He was lonely and poor. He was homesick, too hot, dying of leukaemia, and he flooded his Third Piano Concerto with light. For 40 years, Bartók had been thinking about what folk music might mean to new classical composition – not just plonking a traditional tune in the hands of an orchestra, which plenty of composers had done and still do with varying degrees of care and crassness, but how the most intricate nuances of that tune might shape the sinew and the essential ethos of musical modernism. Bartók didn't pretend it was a simple transaction. He grappled for a lifetime with how to bridge a divide which he'd often found really awkward. Part of it was a class thing. He was acutely self-conscious that his own perceived status as a city intellectual set him at a remove from the musicians he desperately wanted to connect with, whose "authenticity" – big word – he wanted to be a part of. Now he was 7,000 km away from those musicians, their villages, their traditions, their centuries of inherited knowledge. He was dying and Europe was wrecked. Mourning all that, he didn't plonk a folk tune into the hands of an orchestra. He wrote the distilled, luminous hymn that is the slow movement of his *Piano Concerto No. 3*.

On social media I stumbled across a video called "classical versus folk". A string quartet is playing Mozart's *Eine kleine Nachtmusik*. The musicians are besuited and polished, then one of the violinists reaches into a bag, pulls out a woodsy straw hat with a big wide brim and places it on the head of the other violinist, who proceeds to "folk it up". He kicks out his legs and makes his playing all scratchy in a sort of hammed-up hoedown. The audience finds it hilarious. Bartók would have been utterly depressed.

Mercifully I haven't been able to track down that video again, but classical music is hooked on these sort of hoedown equivalents that make kitsch fodder out of tradition. In works old and new, large and small, that contrived and self-conscious capital-letter Folksiness crops up in concert halls all the time. My hunch is that in Scotland we get the worst of it because our repertoire of traditional tunes is magnificent and considered up for grabs – or maybe we lean into it more gamely because we have centuries of practice when it comes to capitalising on tartan tat. What's interesting is thinking about a time before genre divisions got in the way, and how Scotland can now get it right. We've produced plenty of sonic doggerel that passes for "folk-inspired", but we've also made some of the most beautiful and meaningful points of intersection – music that comes exhilaratingly close to Bartók's ideal of modernism with roots deep in the soil.

The distinction between "classical" and "folk" music only really emerged in the late eighteenth and into the nineteenth centuries. The words only make sense (to the extent they do) when they're set in opposition to each other. The musicologist Matthew Gelbart has written a terrific book on the subject called *The Invention of Folk Music and Art Music*, in which he details how it used to be that musicians just played music: what mattered was place and purpose, not so much who wrote the tune or who played it or how they spoke. The same musicians would cover courts, pop songs and worship. These musicians travelled and shape-shifted. If dancing was required, they would play dance standards. If the mood was contemplative, they would unravel something slow and soulful.

Scotland is a key protagonist in what became a global business of musical binaries, and John Knox has much to answer for. A violin and a fiddle were two words for the same thing – and they might have stayed that way had Knox not been outraged by a gathering he witnessed in Orléans where "fidling and flynging" – music and dancing – were apparently gateway drugs leading straight to mass adultery. Sounds like quite the party. Back in Scotland, Knox preached against "fiddlers" and the word started to be used in the derogatory, suggesting a musician of lower status, while "violer" became the term of choice for professional gentleman musicians who wore finer breeks and favoured foreign tunes above local ones.

The new dichotomy took a long while to settle. When the 18-year-old Mary Queen of Scots returned to Edinburgh on 19 August 1561, she was treated to an impromptu serenade beneath her window on her first night at Holyrood by (according to her biographer Brantôme, who was prone to playing fast and loose with numbers) "some five or six hundred scoundrels of the town". Story goes that this scratch band "gave her a serenade with wretched violins and little rebecs [*meschants violons et petits rebecs*] of which there is no lack in Scotland, to which they chanted psalms so badly sung and so out of tune that nothing could be worse. Ha!" Right? I would pay serious money to restage that proto-Fluxus rabble of fiddles and raucous psalm singers. And while Brantôme wasn't too impressed, what he captured there was a crux moment in musical history. In the mix that night beneath Mary's window alongside the scoundrels and the psalm singers were royal "violers", who still knew the same tunes as everyone else. Lines of distinction had been drawn, but the ink had not yet dried.

Two centuries later, in 1771, Robert Fergusson published his "Elegy, on the Death of Scots Music":

> Now foreign sonnets bear the gree,
> And crabbit queer variety
> Of sound fresh sprung frae Italy,
> A bastard breed!
> Unlike that saft-tongu'd melody
> Which now lies deid.

Was Fergusson really so hostile to foreign culture? Probably not, given he befriended the star Italian castrato Tenducci in Edinburgh and Tenducci sang Fergusson's words set to old Scottish tunes at the Theatre Royal, Canongate. In the poem Fergusson mourns the death in 1756 of composer William McGibbon: a man who published three collections of *Scots Tunes* for fiddle but was also principal violinist of the Edinburgh Musical Society and happily inhabited exactly those sounds "fresh sprung frae Italy" that Fergusson skewers. James Oswald was another excellent chameleon, flitting from dance bands in Fife to Court Composer to King George III. Oswald died two years before Fergusson published his "Elegy". If the poem has been read as xenophobic, I'd suggest a subtler point: that Fergusson wasn't so much lamenting the arrival of international music, but the close of a chapter when local music was breathed in the same breath. Over in Edinburgh's New Town, the building work had just begun. Robert Louis Stevenson was a son of the New Town but he preferred the Old, where all walks of life jostled literally on top of each other in the tenements. The New Town was designed to demarcate, and Stevenson bemoaned its "draughty parallelograms".

Through the nineteenth century, Scotland's formal musical institutions were formed, orchestras were founded, concert halls were built to house them and middle classes grew to frequent them, and so real and perceived borders were constructed around certain kinds of music and what they seemed to signify. High and low, salaried and hand-to-mouth, formally educated and self-taught, literate and ear-trained, posh and working class. Classical and folk. Take every one of those terms with an enormous pinch of salt. Arnold Schoenberg – Austrian composer, theorist and atonal paterfamilias – talked about "the wall separating folk music from art". These things were like "petroleum and olive oil," he said, "or ordinary water and holy water".

Schoenberg's Old Vienna attitude still lingers in many nations where class systems exist and culture has been coopted and in some cases weaponised to guard those lines of hierarchy. What complicates the picture in Scotland is the shortbread tin. The keen market kickstarted by eighteenth-century romantics who loved the image of the wild kilted Highlander standing on a hill brandishing a set of bagpipes or, yes, a fiddle. Matthew Gelbart writes about the breathlessness of eighteenth-century Europeans in search of the exotic "other" – how, once they'd drunk the Ossianic Kool-aid, they didn't have to look so far to get their exotic kicks. These coveted "others" were right there on their rocky European coastlines, conveniently dressed as handsome primitives. In Scotland we happily traded that stereotyping for tourism. We still do.

Which maybe explains why generations of classical composers have simultaneously patronised and idealised notions of Scottish folk music while plugging it into their own work in an attempt to conjure some deeper sense of ruggedness and belonging. I won't name names – I would get into trouble – but it's easy to hear who has appropriated, pinched and parodied. They might call it celebrating, honouring, polishing, elevating – there are many terms for what happens in the process, most of them loaded with the implication of new and improved status (it's insinuated) when any music enters the concert hall. The original source often gets little or very generalised credit. In the classical world, I still encounter a lingering sense that folk music is of the earth and therefore folk musicians must be of the earth too, like trees budding music as naturally as leaves. Or stones that have always just been there.

Having said no names: Felix Mendelssohn deserves special mention for his overture *The Hebrides*. For nearly 200 years, those ten brooding minutes of B minor have been promoted as pure-drop West Coast glowering skies, those choppy phrases an evocation of Hebridean spume on basalt and whatnot. There's a giddy pride that one of Germany's big-deal composers graced our shores and, what's more, immortalised his visit in music. Earlier this year, the Scottish Chamber Orchestra opened a concert at Glasgow's Celtic Connections with the Hebrides Overture before showcasing actual folk musicians performing orchestral arrangements of their own music. It was an awkward choice, as though needing to validate the concert with a "proper" classical work. Mendelssohn did make a three-week tour of Scotland when he was 20 in 1829, but he was too seasick to get off the boat in Fingal's Cave and he hated everything about our traditional music. "Ten thousand evils take all folkishness!" he wrote, calling the music he heard during his travels "infamous, vulgar, out-of-tune trash... bellowed out by rough, nasal voices, accompanied with awkward bungling fingers." Not a fan, then.

On the other hand, Benjamin Franklin, founding father of the United States, came to his own heavily romanticised conclusions about why Scottish traditional music felt to him so perfect. In 1759 and 1771, Franklin spent time soaking up the Scottish Enlightenment in Edinburgh, playing chess and drinking porter at a Cowgate club called Lucky Middlemass's Tavern. He decided the reason he loved the music he heard was that it must have been written by bards of old, who would have sat by the fire working out tunes on a harp. And because harp strings keep ringing after being twanged, the tunesmiths needed to write melodies whose notes worked alongside each other – thus providing a special "natural" quality to their harmonic sequences. Regardless of the questionable rigour of this argument, or the implication that anything deviating from tonality becomes "unnatural" and therefore unwelcome, I'm including this story because I love that an American diplomat bothered to form any opinion at all about the uniqueness of implied harmonies in the traditional music of a foreign country. And it's telling: Franklin's theory fit snugly with the picturesque image of the intuitive Scottish musician, improvising by the hearth, at one with nature.

According to the composer Chris Newman, there are two ways of making music. Either you write about real experience, or you send a postcard. Don't send postcards. Which isn't to imply staying clear of the intersection I'm discussing: it just has to come from an honest place. For composer Michael Finnissy, meaningful connection with folk music is about acknowledging yearning. "Beethoven was interested in folksong," says Finnissy, "because he found its shapes intriguing and sexy, not for reasons of nationalistic fervour and not simply arranging them for money." Erik Chisholm, born in Glasgow in 1904, is still one of the finest Scottish composers to have woven the form and fabric of folk music into his works. Try his *Piobaireachd Concerto*, or his spare and elegant settings of airs from the Patrick Macdonald collection – Patrick Macdonald being an eighteenth-century minister who travelled Highlands collecting tunes and Gaelic song.

Or try the work of David Fennessy, an Irish composer living in Glasgow, whose Hirta Rounds for string orchestra is as close as I've heard to wind and soil in sound. Hirta is an island in the St Kilda archipelago whose last inhabitants were evacuated in the 1930s, but Fennessy doesn't try to trigger that melancholy by borrowing an old tune. His music has a more abstract sense of time frozen and culture abandoned. He wanted "to find a deeper pulse", he says. "Like the ground or the sea or the mountains. A deep pulse that is felt rather than counted. Everything in a constant state of organic breathing in and out."

Or try Cassandra Miller, who also thrives on breath and who writes the sort of music that emerges when you make yourself vulnerable. It's a subversive thing to do when the dominant version of classical music still venerates gloss and heroism. Miller recently wrote a guitar concerto called *Chanter* for Edinburgh's Dunedin Consort and guitarist Sean Shibe, taking as her starting point another air from the Patrick MacDonald collection. It's worth dwelling on Miller's process, as she describes it:

> One afternoon, Sean Shibe visited my apartment and sang along to the music of Scottish smallpipes player Brìghde Chaimbeul. I recorded his singing, and layered his voice many times on itself — he then sang along to his own recorded voice again and again, reclining on the sofa, until he was somewhere between sleep and song: sleep-chanting. [...] I've taken the sleep-recording of Sean, and I accurately transcribed his sighing to form the skeletal architecture for the guitar part of this concerto. I returned also to the recorded performance of Brìghde, stealing the original ornaments, and exploring how these could inspire the guitar to warble-ripple in its own resonance.

Miller acknowledges her theft, but she adds this blink-and-you-miss-it sentence which I suspect is key to why her treatment of folk music feels so right, and to the broader questions I've been pondering in this essay. "Small truth-window moments of the melody can be heard in the string ensemble, as occasional shafts of richly-coloured light."

Truth-window: an opening in the surface of a wall, revealing the layers inwith.

Kate Molleson is a music journalist who regularly presents BBC Radio 3 programmes including Breakfast, Music Matters *and* Afternoon Concert.

A writer for The Guardian *and* The Herald, *she also contributes to* Opera, Gramophone *and* BBC Music Magazine *and was commissioning editor of* Dear Green Sounds, *a history of Glasgow's music venues commissioned by UNESCO.*

Her radio documentaries (BBC Radio 4, BBC World Service) include a portrait of Ethiopian nun/pianist/composer Emahoy Tsegué-Maryam Guèbrou and a two-part feature on Mongolian opera.

She grew up in various parts of Scotland and the far north of Canada and studied clarinet performance at McGill University (Montreal) and musicology at King's College London, where she researched the operas of Ezra Pound. She was a copy editor, music critic and cycling columnist for the Montreal Gazette *and deputy editor of* Opera *magazine before moving home to Scotland as the* Guardian's *classical music critic in 2010. She lives in Glasgow.*

WEEKEND AT BERNIE'S:
A SURVEY OF RECENT SCOTTISH THEATRE

David Greig

Again a great question demanding to be asked ...

I write as the year turns, and it feels like Scottish Theatre has every reason to feel optimistic. After six years closed, the famous Glasgow Citizens Theatre is shortly to reopen with more seats and better facilities. Alan Cumming has been announced to take over Pitlochry Festival Theatre, an intriguing appointment with star power that could bring the likes of Tilda Swinton or Brian Cox to the most beautifully located theatre in Britain. The Lyceum, from which I depart as Artistic Director in April, will be taken over by James Brining from Leeds Playhouse. James is an acute director with the popular touch. With his artistic nous and administrative rigour, he can be expected to take the Lyceum to new heights. This autumn, audience data suggests that numbers are finally coming back after COVID.

And, in January, a major and much-delayed funding round will finally take place. Until recently all indications were that it would see up to half of theatre companies cut, but UK Labour's surprisingly capacious budget meant that, through the magic of the Barnett Formula, a £3.4 billion increase for The Scottish Government led in turn to a record £34 million increase in the culture budget; and so we approach new year with a shade less dread. All in all, Hogmanay 2024 should have seen the cheerful clinking of cheap prosecco at the annual gatherings of the hard-pressed theatricals.

But, in truth, the hopeful turn can't hide the grim effects of a lost decade during which Scottish Theatre was repeatedly battered by austerity, Brexit, COVID, inflation, local authority cuts, and the cumulative effect of eighteen years of standstill funding. This Christmas it felt to many as though the institution we had called "Scottish Theatre" was, in fact, dead – and that we, the theatre managers, were farcically dragging its corpse around from party to party like the characters in *Weekend at Bernie's*.

Scottish Theatre was born in 1967 when the visionary Labour Minister Jennie Lee expanded the Arts Council's funding to Scotland. Until that point, what theatre there was had mostly been variety shows, amateur players, and touring work brought in from London. Lee, a working class left-winger who had been brought up above a music hall in Cowdenbeath, took the Fabian ideology of the Arts Council – which had been created to protect high culture from the populism of a proletarian government – and turned that logic on its head. For Lee, high culture belonged to everyone, and so it must be offered to everyone. She saw that, for art to have its full transformative power, it must also be made in the places it would be seen; in the wake of her reforms, a network of fully funded producing theatre buildings and companies was established in Scotland.

Theatre was a big part of the late twentieth-century renaissance of Scottish culture. Growing up in Edinburgh in the 80s, I don't remember a great deal of difference between the theatre habits of Unionists and nationalists. "Scottish Theatre" was ours and it needed looking after. It was the unique and fragile outgrowth of this rocky Atlantic archipelago, its motley peoples and its peculiar history.

It could get silly. I remember, after the premier of David Harrower's Knives in Hens at The Traverse in 1995 there was a lengthy debate in the bar about the play's peculiar idiolect. Was it Scots? Was it English? In the gents I happened to stand next to Simon Donald, author of *The Life of Stuff*. He turned to me and muttered, "Two Scottish writers having a pish, but is it Scottish pish, that's the real question."

Alasdair Gray wrote in *Lanark* that a city doesn't really exist until it's been written about in a novel. In the same way it's possible that a national culture doesn't really exist until its domestic life has been represented on stage, until it has its own Hamlet, until there's been a translation of Chekhov. This was always the unstated purpose of Scottish Theatre – to conjure us into being.

The energy in Scottish Theatre was a small part of what brought devolution into being in 1997; but ironically, that very success brought with it a problem: now we really exist, so why do we still need to fund theatre? So that audiences can have cheap tickets? For moral improvement? To show off?

It's worth noting that this is partly about language. In Estonia or Latvia, it simply wouldn't be a question; but in Scotland, we know that London and New York will continue to provide us with all the English language theatre we need, at a reasonable price and in perpetuity, without the need for any public support at all.

During the Blairite years, when times were comparatively good, no one in government saw any need to approach this difficult question. Both Labour and SNP were able to proceed on the happy principle that culture is a jolly good thing, doesn't cost us much anyway. On you go lads, do whatever it is you do and send us the photographs for our website when you're done.

Then in 2010 a Quango called Creative Scotland took over arts funding, its vague name a symptom of this unwillingness to define terms. Without a guiding ideology everything became a priority: grassroots work, subversive work, new work, revivals, minority languages, the touring and the site-specific. It was vital that funding embraced new technologies, but it was also vital that we stayed in touch with our traditional forms. We must tour internationally and also to the highlands... Is it Scottish? Is it Creative? Fund it!

After the financial crash this caravan hit the brick wall of austerity. With suddenly diminishing resources, there was a clear need either for more money or less work – but without a clear sense as to *why*, it proved impossible for either the Scottish Government or Creative Scotland to develop a strategy. Artistic merit isn't measurable in numbers, so in their absence grant application forms became longer, with more and more varied means of assessing value: environmental impact, social justice, fair pay, community work, and international visibility. Despite the onerous non-artistic work involved in meeting these targets, none of it served to provide an answer to which work should be supported and which should not.

To be fair, whenever Creative Scotland did try to make an actual decision, it would invariably provoke what's called in Scotland "a stushie": a wave of online criticism and articles in the press. Often this was because the decision was wrong, but either way, the Scottish Government, eager to avoid bad publicity, would put pressure on CS, and the decision would end up being reversed.

We were left in the somewhat absurd situation where, instead of an arms-length funding body protecting artists from government, we saw the government called upon to protect artists from the arms-length funder.

Theatre funding was, in effect, frozen at a standstill and allowed to shrink slowly over time via inflation: a process which has drained money away from the core at an alarming rate. At first producing theatres increased ticket prices. Then dynamic pricing came in to wring as much as possible out of the core audience. Play choices became more conservative. But the shortfalls grew.

Companies began to co-produce. This shared costs but forced even safer artistic choices. Freelancers also took a hit, as it effectively halved the overall number of shows being made. And still the shortfalls grew.

The next solution was to increase income from donors. Over my time at the Lyceum, we moved from a donated income of around £70,000 to well over £600,000. And still the shortfalls grew. Jobs were cut, shows were cut, cast sizes were cut, and work shrivelled away.

In a rare positive moment, George Osborne introduced Theatre Tax Relief. This scheme gives back a portion of any show's production costs to its maker after the premiere. TTR requires no forms, no gatekeeping and no work beyond the submission of accounts. It now stands at 40%, and it's the single factor which makes it viable for theatres in Scotland to make a new show rather than take in touring work from London. It's an acid irony that while Labour and the SNP both boasted about their love of Scotland's culture it was a Tory, Westminster policy which ended up throwing Scottish Theatre a lifeline.

And that's when COVID struck. Audience shrinkage, inflation and the peculiar self-imposed disaster of the Truss budget were a series of baseball-bat blows to a sector still struggling to get off its knees. We, the artists, also seemed lost. The high culture Jennie Lee had fought so hard to share was now regarded as a problem. Making a play simply in order divine a truth about the world came to seem old-fashioned, indulgent or mainstream.

The decade saw a burgeoning in "ought-to" theatre: work created not because anyone demanded to make it, or because an audience demanded to see it, but because someone somewhere felt it *ought* to be made. We *ought* to do a Scottish play. We *ought* to commission a writer from this or that category. We *ought* to cover this important topic. Often just, we *ought* to tick this or that box for Creative Scotland. Unfortunately, the shows produced often just told an audience, in a fairly straightforward way, what they ought to think. I'm in no position to point fingers. I've written and produced a fair amount of *ought to* work myself.

A friend who stood as a candidate for the SNP once told me that, during COVID, when they couldn't canvas door to door, their policy ideas became increasingly weird; it was only once they started to canvas in person again that they realised who the electorate were, and what issues actually concerned them. It's the same in theatre. Separated from our audience, we drifted into an East German culture of plays about state-approved topics, often resulting in the audience feeling either bored, lectured or castigated, and sometimes all three; they could get enough of that at home.

Despite these obstacles, much excellent theatre has been made in Scotland recently – a testament to my colleagues in every part of the industry who have pushed water uphill every day to make any work happen at all. Oran Mor, the lunchtime pub theatre in the West End of Glasgow, has developed into a well-oiled machine for producing new plays. The format: twenty plays a season, two or three handers which last for precisely 45 minutes can, in the hands of writers such as Douglas Maxwell or Lesley Hart, be clever, funny and-up-to-the-minute: the theatrical equivalent of a short story.

Elizabeth Newman's tenure as Artistic Director at Pitlochry brought an expansive new attitude to what had been a rather staid theatre in the Highlands. During the pandemic, she built an outdoor amphitheatre set in woodland above the Tummel River, the first to be built in Scotland since 80 AD. Elizabeth also supervised the building of a new indoor studio theatre in which she staged a series of new plays by emerging Scottish writers. Newman is one of a clutch of women writers and directors who commanded our big stages with strong theatrical visions: at the Lyceum, Wils Wilson had a string of proscenium-busting productions of classics, notably *Life is a Dream*. Zinnie Harris forged a new role as writer-director taking apart classic female roles such as Duchess of Malfi and Lady Macbeth and revisioning them. She also wrote and directed the mordant, sorrowful, couple-comedy *Scent of Roses*. Gabriel Quigley's *Girls of Slender Means* was an Edinburgh smash.

Francis Poet, whose new musical about Lockerbie will re-open the Citz, wrote the darkly funny asbestos drama *Fibres*. Hannah Lavery's *Lament for Sheku Bayoh* with music by Heir of the Cursed and The Young Fathers was a plangent memorial to a man who died in police custody. Morna Pearson's *Dracula* and Morna Young's *Sunset Song*, brought Scots as a dramatic language into the twenty-first century and Linda Maclean's poetic voice found expression in *Castle Lennox*, a glorious, heart-filling musical about the end of the asylum system in Scotland, performed by the Lung Ha Ensemble of actors with learning difficulties. Cora Bisset continued her long run of popular hits with *What Girls are Made Of* and she took a bold swing at a homegrown Glasgow musical with her surreal adaptation of Peter Mullan's *Orphans*.

The standout writer-director of the period was surely Isabel MacArthur, whose 2018 hit *Pride and Prejudice (sort of)* was the decade's most influential production. A re-telling of Austen's novel presented by five female servants in an imaginary country house, set to a soundtrack of 1970s disco, it hit home with Scottish audiences, toured around Britain and was commercially presented in the West End. The play is still running on tour, and features on The Queen Mary's Atlantic crossings, making it possibly the most commercially successful Scottish show ever.

Throughout the decade Rona Munro made her history cycle *The James Plays*: an ambitious attempt to portray the entire Stuart Dynasty. It's fair to say that the average Scot knows more about English kings than Scots ones, so Munro, as well as writing six terrific large-scale plays, has also shone a light on our own clattering history. I do hope someone will stage them all in a festival so they can be seen for what they really are: one of the great achievements of Scottish Theatre.

Another writer of breathtaking ambition is David Ireland. With plays like *Cyprus Avenue* and *Ulster American* he became one of the most important voices in British playwriting, writing razor-sharp Shavian moral dilemmas, couched within bleakly farcical comedy and pointedly un-woke language. It's interesting that David is simultaneously a Northern Irish playwright, an Irish playwright, a British playwright and a Scottish playwright. His emergence during this period is perhaps a reflection of the peculiarly unsettled modern identities in these islands. He's a writer whose work speaks clearly to every one of those four polities and yet, somehow, he seems fully at home in none of them.

Another positive has been the increased ethnic and linguistic diversity (including British Sign Language) of our workforce. In part, this is the happy result of an influx of New Scots during the 1990s after the UK asylum dispersal policy. Those children now are thoroughly rejuvenating our ranks of talent. The most famous example is probably Ncuti Gatwa, the new Doctor Who, who began his career in Dundee Rep. Looking forward, the children of New Scots from Poland, Latvia, Lithuania, Estonia and Ukraine who settled here in the 2000s will also soon come through, bringing their own stories and perspectives to our stages.

In the midst of all this, the Scottish Independence Referendum – despite being a shattering political event – appears to have produced no significant art. Even now, a full 10 years on, I can't point to any novels, poems, plays or films that make a serious attempt to reflect that extraordinary moment. Somehow, Indyref managed to convulse Scottish society but pass almost unremarked in theatre. Perhaps it was an issue of funding. It's hard to write a state-of-the-nation piece for two actors. But Scottish Independence was always more a continuation of devolution than a grab for "Freedom!" in the Gibsonian sense, its energies more civic than cultural, with an eagerness to embrace internationalism and inclusivity. Noble sentiments, I embrace them myself; but they're not, maybe, the stuff to produce the wild art that makes a nation. All in all, I can't help feeling that devolution has left Scottish culture somewhat adrift. It sometimes feels as if we've all been engaged in a vaguely administrative project, almost as if we were trying to build art from the excitement of redrawing a local authority border.

For me, the best single production of the last five years was Michael Boyd's *Medea* adapted by Liz Lochhead and performed during the Edinburgh Festival of 2022. Liz's adaptation into Scots was already well-regarded but in Michael's revival it re-emerged as a classic: funny, accessible, and yet at the same time, wholly honouring Euripides with furious poetry full of mystery, wisdom, eroticism, and pain. Michael, and designer Tom Piper, put a thrust into the old stone church at The Hub and required the audience to stand around the stage looking up at the god-like royal figures. The NTS' unique funding resource brought us a diverse cast of fourteen, expertly costumed, beautifully lit, led by Adura Onashile in a shamanic turn as Medea: the foreign woman whose response to her husband's betrayal is to murder her children. On the night I saw it, it felt like an adrenaline injection into Scottish Theatre's ailing frame.

A year later, Michael passed away. At his memorial service, we looked back at his reign at the Tron in the 80s, when he turned an old church in Glasgow into a powerhouse of European theatre. Somehow, with decent funding and light-touch bureaucratic accountability, Michael produced dazzling civic and artistic work which would nourish Scotland for years to come. Could anyone look back at The Tron and question its value to the taxpayer? Would more forms have helped? Should its environmental impact have been more of a concern? Was it a problem that Michael was privately educated? Or that he was part Northern Irish, part Scots, part English?

Michael made theatre wholly of and for its moment because he was an artist to his bones – he did the work his gut demanded – and by doing so he shaped all of us who followed him, including the failures. As Michael once said to me: "if your theatre never fails then you're not taking enough risks."

I remain optimistic. 2025 is a turning of the wheel. Arts funding in Scotland is to be "reviewed" by Government which surely must offer the chance for priorities to emerge. Change is coming. I can see it in the talented Scottish actors, writers, musicians and poets who are making work on their own, outside the system, often for no money. I see it in the determination of the more established theatre-makers to remain, fight and push boundaries even when it would be easier to work in television or to move south. Most of all I feel it because the world is once again a great question demanding to be asked. Something new is about to be born on our stages; I know it.

But for now, this Hogmanay, I raise my cheap prosecco with the toast: "Scottish Theatre is dead; long live Scottish Theatre."

David Greig is a playwright and theatre-maker from Edinburgh. He was appointed Artistic Director of The Lyceum Theatre in Edinburgh in 2015 and will be leaving his post to return to writing in 2025.

AN ECOLOGY OF HAUNTING: RE-FORMING A FUTURE FROM SCOTLAND'S PAST

Margaret Elphinstone

The new Clearances.

The history of a nation is formed by constantly re-seeding words and giving them whatever new meanings the times require. Wherever a story starts, there has to be a back story to give a bearing for the plot to follow. The land offers the long view. Outlines shift in and out of focus. I stand at Carlin's Cairn on Galloway's Rhinns of Kells. I face south to the great hump of the Corserine where the ancient passes crossed before these hills became the road to nowhere. Here on Carlin's Cairn summit I think of the Carlin – the old woman – for whom this massive cairn is named. Some say she was the miller's wife at Polmaddy who sheltered Robert the Bruce; some say she was the Gaelic Mother Goddess, who sheltered everybody. Embedded in her name is a suggestion of singularity; in fact the Carlin is a thrawn auld besom. Yet this same Carlin confers legendary power and enables magical transformations.

The Carlin has a fine, all-encompassing view from up here. She sees changes hurtle down the ages like an unstoppable tidal wave. Land under a kilometre of ice harbours nothing sentient. Only nunataks like Ben Lawers in the eastern Highlands, islanded above the ice sheet, hold on to scraps of life. As the weight of ice lifts off the land, the sea rises. Beaches are stranded high and dry in one place; sea sweeps the soil away in another. As the ice melts, life comes back: tundra, scrub, flowers, trees, birds and insects, little animals and at last the great herbivores. The hunters follow. The hunters have names for everything, to the very edge of their awareness. Place names record moments of habitation, a bit of rock and water briefly colonised by language. In due course the land will be uninhabited again, but the hunters have no words for that.

The glen where I live is bounded to the west by the Rhinns of Kells. The Rhinns mark the edge of the Galloway Hills, historically the haunt of outlaws, gipsies, smugglers and Covenanting rebels. Now the passes are blocked by ranks of Sitka spruce, one of the monumental conifers of the American West Coast, crushed into an arboreal Gulag in the Scottish hills. The ridge itself is clear of plantation, and now, strangely, rowan seedlings have settled themselves all over the bare summits, thriving in the face of feral goats and deer. Is this some kind of come-back?

At any given time the dominant narrative imposes its imperious boundaries. Place names like Carlin's Cairn, marooned in time, subvert the story. I think of the hills and coasts of Rùm, where there are few place names and the map is disconcertingly empty. Everyone except one family was evicted in 1825. When people leave, their words leave with them. What, for example, did the expelled islanders call Bloodstone Hill, where, when the ice retreated, hunter gatherers collected the curious blue bloodstone from which they made their blades? On Bloodstone Hill I weighed one of these stones in my hand. I studied its bluish sheen, its blemishes like the eyes in a potato. I looked up the empty glen. Over the pass, on the east coast of Rùm, the Mesolithic arrivals made their camps. Through the great length of years people kept on moving; the subjects kept changing. Now the nineteenth-century deerstalkers' grotesque mansion stands empty. A new community, who finally own their island, lives round the bay where the ferry comes in. But all the time I was on Rùm I felt something was missing.

And now I'm on the summit of Mullach na Dheirigan above Glen Mullardoch as the mist clears. From the north-east edge of a sweeping horseshoe I look across across the great corrie to Sgurr nan Ceathreamhan. My eyes follow it round until it drops away to the Iron Lodge. I face west into the wind and see ridge upon ridge like long waves, right to the far-off Cuillin. These Highland mountains feel like wilderness, and yet, traversing the deserted glens, I'm constantly aware of people who are no longer here. They've left rickles of stones and the lines of field systems, and something else, a sense of habitation. I see it in the lush grass, nettles and buttercups around the ruined clachans. Later I look at the Chisholm Cairn of the Five Continents at the entrance to Glen Mullardoch, made up of stones brought by visiting Chisholms of the diaspora. A desert is not a wilderness, but people like me, who do not belong to these glens, enjoy it as if it were primeval, untouched land. It is not.

Shadows race across the glen, driven by winds which don't reach down here. Meanings cast fleeting shadows too: to inhabit, to occupy, to colonise. I inhabit my country moment by moment, as impressions, nearly all lost to conscious memory, succeed one another in an unbroken thread. To inhabit a place is to become part of it. I also occupy this country, and that constitutes something different. It's no longer timeless: it indicates a moment of arrival, and therefore, departure. Occupation implies displacement of something other:

a pristine wilderness or someone else's home. The history I was taught came in the form of wave upon wave of occupations, driven by some intangible notion of progress, which somewhere along the line became entangled with an ideology of economic growth. I colonise this country – no, I don't want to write that. But I can't avoid the fact that the people who once lived in this glen are gone, and now I, a stranger, can pitch my tent wherever I like, and make myself at home.

In the first Clearances the people were replaced by sheep. Two hundred years of these hungry immigrants – sheep are not native to Scotland – have turned our uplands into what ecologists call wet deserts. Not a desert of the heart, however, and still alive in memories, often shared in song, music and story. As a childhood visitor – never an inhabitant – to the world of hill-farming, what I remember most is the sheepy smell, clinging to muck and byre and boots and caddy lambs by the Rayburn. A world of extremes, but the hellish side was hidden from me. I remember a dead sheep with maggots in it but I don't remember seeing anyone do their accounts. Hill farms can't pay. Selling up? Poetry, not pounds, puts true value on it: "my words will never fill his run-down barn, / my lines cannot defend his fragile land," (Jim Carruth, *Killochries*).

The hills and glens of this hungry, wet land are being bought by investors from other countries and planted with conifers. Conifer agents lobby for grants and tax breaks, plan for profits after 30 years, then offshore millions in cash. Organic and outdoor farmers are refused support, and must move on. We're trapped in a brutal procession of evictions. I prefer to believe there is space here for all of us.

There would be space, were it not stolen. I walk through the village in Galloway where I live. Broken bits of wall, grass-grown bumps where whins and hawthorn force their way through, a jagged gable end, write our story on the land. There was once a road here; now a muddy path winds between fallen stones and humped middens. A couple of roe deer leap across the path and run between the ruins. Kites circle against blue sky. There's not a soul in sight. Fields and gardens are gone. Nothing grows in the stifling dark under the close-ranked spruce. But it hasn't happened to my village yet. The clachans of the Upper Dee have vanished under plantations, but today, here in the Glenkens, I walk past lighted houses, even if local people can't afford to live in them. I cross green fields, even if local people can't have any land to grow their food. I pass the school, which might stay for a while if some young families find anywhere to live. In ten years time I might still be able to buy a drink somewhere around here. But don't count on it. The twenty-first century Clearances are happening faster than we think.

Other Clearances are happening furth of Scotland, as brutal as any that occurred here, and ultimately springing from the same source. People far from Scotland are being forced from their land in a process driven by climate change and shaped, just as the post-industrial Scottish Clearances were, by land hunger, war, expanding global markets and corporate greed. Often these new inhabitants arrive here with nothing except memories of the land they have lost. In a seminar room in Glasgow I listen to laments for orchard oases rich in apricots and pomegranates; for the shared plenty of the olive harvest; for okra at the succulent heart of every dish; for the last pristine forest in Europe, now bisected by a brutal wall; I read of a spring where a girl fetched water every day, stooping over a clear pool shaded by a fig tree. When the fig was cut down for a palm oil plantation, the pool had no shade, and the spring that had sustained a village vanished too.

Displacement means losing the land you live on, your family and neighbours, the very food you eat. I take a friend to the ridge of Sgurr Thium above Glenfinnan to show him my country. I spread out my arms to take in the Highland hills, my expansive vision of ridge upon stony ridge disappearing into endless blue. He looks round slowly. "But this place is a desert," he says, "Why do no birds sing?"

Here in the Glenkens, the curlews used to come back in April, swooping across the field above the Crockett Memorial where Stevenson's words are inscribed: "Where about the graves of the martyrs the whaups are crying / His heart remembers how." I too have my memories. I remember the peewits and plovers on the moor, ubiquitous larks, whirring kestrels, the swifts who nested under the eaves of every house in our street so short a time ago. I remember the sea cliffs on Foula: rank upon rank of birds, from shags on the skerries below, gannets above the tideline, serried tenements of guillemots, razorbills, rock doves, kittiwakes, fulmars, the puffins nesting on the cliff-tops, rafts of murmuring eiders dotting the white-threaded sea beyond the rocks. I remember ptarmigan and snow bunting on snow-covered mountains in the all-embracing cold. I remember the blackbird who nested in the ragged elder at the gate of our Glasgow drying green. I beat on the window while the incoming magpies smashed the nest and scattered yellow yolks across our gate. The magpies moved on when starving gulls came inland to nest on tenement ledges and pockle food from dustbins. "Why do no birds sing?" Memory is elegy. In a world turned desert, you either die or move on.

Every day we lose a little more of the land we live on. Like the Fisher King of the Waste Lands, we're living in an encroaching desert and we can't break the spell that binds us. This cannot be the way to live. Far from Scotland, indigenous voices tell the world that there are better ways for people to inhabit their land. Here at home we are still surrounded by other, non-human lives. If the lands and seas of Scotland belong to anyone, they belong to these other living beings. They, not we, are truly indigenous. They have the right to remain unmolested, and not to have their habitations torn to pieces around them. They own nothing; they have no voices that we can hear. To name them is at least an acknowledgement of their presence.

I keep watch. The land offers the close view. A hare crosses my path without spotting me; it bounds away up the field with longlegged grace. Young oak leaves make freckled shadows under trees much older than this wood. Today's sunshine brings out a lizard. It wriggles through short grass and rests against the warmth of rock. Eyes bright and alert, tiny hand-like claws, skin greenish-smooth, striped like the grass that hid it. Its tail is a stump: whatever happened, the lizard escaped with its life. Its unawareness of my presence is like a veil drawn back. I'm looking straight into another life, of far older stock than mine but undiminished. People have a language for this other place we can never quite inhabit: words like "nature" and "wild" which define our sense of loss rather than the independent sentience of other lives. This lizard is as alive as I am. I don't want any part in a country in which it has nowhere left to go.

West of Carlin's Cairn there are few paths and almost no walkers; an Australian mining company covets the minerals that lie beneath the hills. To the south is the Silver Flow, a watery world of blanket bogland like no other left in this country. Sitka seedlings are colonising its wetlands; the waters are threatened by plantation run-off. To the east lies the proposed route of the giant pylons which will rip through the between-lands of this glen – uplands where oaks, ash and beech once gave gradual way to rowan, birch and hazel, then bog myrtle and heather. The burns fall from the hills to spread into pools and rivers, down to the glens where people make their lives. The more hard-line the boundaries, the more the between-lands become expendable. They lie at the distant mercy of alien money.

Marginal lands, like the border between ice and forest, are by definition in a constant state of change. Like Carlin's Cairn, they inhabit that unstable space where different possibilities meet. Meanings change boundaries too; "marginal lands" have been re-defined under capitalism as places where it's so hard to wrest a living that its resources can be plundered by anyone, except, usually, its own inhabitants. Other living beings need undisturbed land, and we also need land that sustains our own species. The in-between lands, where human and other living networks merge into one another, are the catalyst for any possible future.

In 1724 the Galloway Levellers fought back against land enclosure and eviction. Near Blates Mill, south of the Mossdale Brig, they tore down the dykes which excluded them from their land. 150 years later, the writer S.R. Crockett was born here: "I can remember the broad spread of the moor over which we had come, the warmth of the shawl in which I was wrapped, the dreamy scent of the newly-cut fir-chips in which they had left me nested ... Such is the first beginning that I remember of that outdoor life, to which ever since my eyes have kept themselves wide-open." I imagine living in a country which offers every one of its children, wherever they came from, such security of habitation.

Today, most of Scotland's land remains in the hands of the absent few. Most wars are fought about land: who owns it and what the boundaries are. Hugh Macmillan's poem "The Hert o The Matter" looks to "the saund fowk, the shaw fowk" who inhabit, but do not own, the place they call home: "there maun be an airt / we can forgaither an cant / we fowk o the hert." Every living thing that inhabits our country needs the fowk o the hert to find new words to speak for the land. The Levellers have not yet won.

In 1948 the Seven Men of Knoydart made their first attempt to reclaim their land. Since 1997 on Eigg, the people who live on the island are the people who own it. Other places have followed: Stornaway, Assynt, Knoydart, Mull of Galloway, Ulva, most recently Langholm Moor, to name only a few. In Edinburgh and Aberdeen there is community-owned land. The places at the edge find the way; the urban heartlands follow.

We inherit a culture recklessly disconnected from the land, and wholly distanced from the remote sources that feed us. When our fragile monetary and political systems collapse, most people will have nothing to eat. We will discover very quickly just who owns what. We could yet use our land kindly and get fed. Some farmers are working with more cattle and fewer sheep. An integrated system with no fences means less work for humans and more chance of survival for other lives. Might then Scotland's nightingales come back; might nightjar and blackcock return to their old homes? Might the dubh lochans fill again, and swarm with dragonflies? There is still hope on the high moors.

On the shores of the Solway Firth the may is out. From the top of a hawthorn a missel thrush is singing its full-throated song. I see it through a gap in the white blossom: speckled brown breast, beady eye, open beak. It must nest here. The firth glints beyond the trees. Over there, across a strip of sea, is England. West of it, the Isle of Man, then Ireland. The tides of the Solway Firth ebb and flow in a perilous between-land of swift current and quaking mudbank. Here on solid ground, the spring grass is sprinkled with lady's-smock, campion and stitchwort. It's just a moment in an ordinary day, but the connection is live. I am aware of the unfathomable history of this place, and of possibilities that may be fulfilled in other lives than mine. Meanwhile I don't want to miss these moments. They are unexpected, sudden, altogether quick. I don't have any time to waste. This is the country I inhabit.

Margaret Elphinstone was educated at Queens College, London, and Durham University, where she graduated in English Language and Literature (B.A. Hons) in 1970. Thereafter she has lived and worked in many parts of Scotland including Glasgow, Shetland, Moray and Galloway.

She published her first futuristic novel in 1987. Her first historical novel, The Sea Road *(Canongate Books, 2000), was published in 2000 and won a Scottish Arts Council Spring Book Award. She is also the author of* Lost People *(Wild Goose Publications, 2004);* The Gathering Night *(Canongate Books, 2009);* Gato *(Sandstone Press, 2007);* Light *(Canongate Books, 2006);* Voyageurs *(Canongate Books, 2003);* Hy Brasil *(Canongate Books, 2002);* Islanders *(Polygon, 1994);* Apple from a Tree *(Women's Press, 1990);* A Sparrow's Flight *(Polygon, 1989); and* The Incomer *(Women's Press, 1987). She has also written two books on organic gardening, short stories, academic articles and poetry. She is a Professor of English Emerita of University of Strathclyde.*

WHERE STANDS GAELIC LITERATURE?

Peter Mackay

Doubleness — with grim undertows.

I have just started reading *Gormshuil an Rìgh* (2010). Again. It is the third time, and I have some hope this time of understanding it, or at least most of it. It is probably the most ambitious Gaelic novel written this century in terms of language and non-linear storytelling; it embeds the shape-shifting quality of older Gaelic tales into a modern "novel" form against which it rails in odd, unexpected ways. And its language is extremely rich, extremely localised. Fionnlagh MacLeòid, the author, was from Adabrock in Ness, the northern tip of the Isle of Lewis, and the novel can almost be read at times as part of a hyper-local conversation with other novelists and short story tellers from Ness — Tormod and Alasdair Caimbeul, Donnchadh Mac Giollìosa — to show off the linguistic fireworks of how Gaelic is / was / may be again (?) spoken in Ness. I am from just down the road, and even for me the language is tough, pulling me in directions I'm unused to.

The linguistic and literary richness is no surprise. Ness is far from being a literary backwater. Fionnlagh MacLeòid's nephew is the successful novelist and playwright Iain Fionnlagh MacLeòid; Tormod and Alasdair Caimbeul were one of the most well-known literary families in the Gàidhealtachd, stretching back three generations (and continuing with Tormod's daughter Catrìona Lexy). Tormod's *Deireadh an Fhoghair* (1979) is widely claimed as the greatest novel ever in Gaelic (though it has been translated to Czech, no English translation exists, so its status in "Scottish" literature is much more shoogily). MacGiollìosa's *Crann-Fige* (2022) won the Highland Book Prize last year as well as the Gaelic Fiction Book of the Year (MacGiollìosa has long lived in London and that distance has helped, in some ways, keep his Gaelic in a state of uncanny placedness). But Ness is also an area very much aware of its edge-ness, and edginess; of the sense of various possible ends of the world: of Autumn coming to an end, as the title of Caimbeul's novel has it [it could be translated as "The End of Autumn"], and of winter being upon us.

In one of Mac Gillìosa's stories, "Am Facal a Chaidh Air Seachran" [The Word that Went Astray] the main character Dòmhnall Iain worries over a word – *a' pèirceanachd, a' pèirceanachd ri rud* – that returns to him one nightfall, while standing at the gable end of his house; this is a word that he can't now remember anyone else using and that exists in no dictionaries. The story as a whole simply sees him speaking to other characters until eventually there is one who has heard it, and can tell him what it means – "trifling, trifling with something" – and he can store it safely with all of the other rare words he has lovingly riffed through in the story, from *stangalanaich* [origins in Norse, meaning "a man, always a man, loitering outside, not doing very much of anything"] to *rùghan*, from *hrúga*, another Old Norse word, for heap. There is very much a sense here of fragments, trifles, stored lovingly against one's ruin.

I've returned to *Gormshuil an Rìgh* because MacLeòid died last year and his widow, Norma – also a novelist and publisher – died a couple of months ago, and I'm rereading whatever of their books I have (plays, short stories, novels), as an act of cairn-building and self-measurement. Both were looming presences, dolmens, in my childhood: friends of both my parents, theirs was a house I was in and out of a few times a year. Both made the very idea of being a "writer" real and almost natural – as long as you had the turn of phrase, the wit. And both had been important figures in the efforts to revive, sustain, resurrect the Gaelic language; efforts that had picked up a head of steam and momentum in the 1970s, and have now given us – me especially – institutions to rely on or take for granted. The publisher that Norma helped found, Acair, publishes my poetry books. I could work as a broadcast journalist at the BBC as a result of the money secured for Gaelic broadcasting in the 1980s and 1990s; I am the external examiner at the Gaelic college, Sabhal Mòr Ostaig, which just celebrated its 50th anniversary with an event at the Parliament in Edinburgh, and a speech from the new First Minister John Swinney, in his first "fun" engagement.

Much has improved in that 50 years: this is the positive slant. There is, though, another perspective. Fionnlagh and Norma lived in Shawbost on Lewis; this village gained some wider attention in the last ten years as the central case study in a 2011 report which highlighted how precarious the continued existence of Gaelic was as a community language in Lewis. This was taken up by a book – *The Gaelic Crisis in the Vernacular Community* – which (rightly) pointed out the serious risk of Gaelic dying out entirely as a community language on the islands while also, in the debate that followed it, creating some tension between different communities of speakers of the languages: island and city, heritage and new speakers. For many Gaelic speakers, none of these discussions are new, though – the question of the survival of the language hovers under the surface of much discussion about the culture, particular during a year, such as this one, when the census figures are released. There is some hope: a marked increase in the overall number of people with some competence in the language. But there is also a grim undertow: for the first time Gaelic is a minority language in the Western Isles, with about 45% of the population speaking the language. Literary concerns and linguistic politics have long been hard to separate in terms of Scottish Gaelic. But is it healthy to think of population sizes when writing about literature, or indeed when writing poems, stories, novels? Is it necessary, unavoidable?

―

Gormshuil an Rìgh is an end-of-the-world novel in its own way. It stages a war between "luchd an sgeul" [the people of the story] and those who would celebrate or enforce "An Leabhar Mòr" [the Big Book]; its terrain is the shifting of an oral tradition – with its fluidity and metamorphic power – into a written one, set down in black and white (ravens make up much of the bookish army). As such it could be read against the *sui generis* works of James Hogg, or the narrative-bending of Flann O'Brien (but without the humour of either). The "luchd an sgeul" are a rag-bag cast of mythological figures. Some – like the title character who could be rendered Greyblue-eye the King – are hyperlocal, some are shape-shifting cyphers (like the "Cèineach" [the distant one]), others are drawn from older tales (Caillte, from *Acallamh na Senórach*, makes an appearance), and one of them is a Chimpanzee called Tommy (the star of the 1987 film *Project X?*). The fact that the novel is creating its own imaginary world, its own tradition as it goes is all to the point – this is, after all, what a vibrant, healthy literature does and can do, unapologetically, and with no easy handholds. But it is perhaps only in such a fantasy world that Gaelic literature can exist so fully in its own realm, its own history, without the incursions of the English language or anglophone culture into its fibre (the acuteness of the situation may in part account for the lack of humour in the novel).

Like *Deireadh an Fhoghair*, *Gormshuil an Rìgh* hasn't been translated into English, and I was very tentative about even offering a translation of the title. It seems a slight betrayal of the novel, of Fionnlagh. This is an odd place in which to be, but perhaps inevitable. As a writer of poems, I can fudge the issue of translation a little bit more than a novelist can: some poems I translate into English, some I don't – some have parallel and divergent lives in both languages (and others). But for novelists like Caimbeul or MacLeòid there are more existential anxieties about the idea of translation; sitting down to write a novel in Gaelic still seems to have a cultural-political force, the decision to choose a particular, precise, and numerically shrinking audience to be an act of resistance. Iain Crichton Smith is the main precursor for contemporary novelists of one who wrote in Gaelic and English (and did his own translations); but his own "doubleness" brought its own anxieties and doubts. And there remains the nagging sense that translation is still one of the main drivers of recognition for Gaelic writers. Would *Crann-Fige* have received some of the awards and attention it did if it wasn't the first of MacGillìosa's books to include English translations? It certainly does him no harm that his remarkable style has a hallucinatory quality that lends itself to translation, and then to being read against short stories in the vein of William Trevor or even Alice Munro; having an English text available of course makes this apparent to more readers ...

There are reasons, in other words, to be depressed, wary, or worried about the state of Gaelic literature, many tied up with the decline of the "vernacular community", with the loss of writers who possess a richness and depth of vocabulary and imagination, or connected to the lurking presence of English-language echoes and shadows. But there are also reasons to be heartened. (Even the focus on the "ends" itself can be heartening: there is always something sneakily reassuring about an imagined apocalypse – it means that the real end-of-the-world is still some way off). Some of this comes from the other side of those census figures.

Much of the best, most interesting, most ambitious poetry and fiction in Gaelic in recent decades has been written by people who have learnt the language as adults, who were not part of that "vernacular community": poets such as Meg Bateman, Christopher Whyte, Fearghas MacFhionnlaigh, Niall O'Gallagher, Deborah Moffat, Beth Frieden; novelists such as Alison Lang, Dàibhidh Eyre, Shelagh Chaimbeul. Indeed, getting, as I do, to judge book and poem competitions, I'm delighted to discover new writers each year from all over the world: *some* of them I can't even guess who they are. And these books gain widespread recognition. Last year's Saltire Awards (Scotland's national literary awards) shortlisted *Polaris*, a poetry collection by Marcas Mac an Tuairneir (originally from York), while loose translations by another Gaelic learner Taylor Strickland (originally from the US) of the nineteenth-century poet Alasdair mac Mhaighstir Alasdair, *Dastrum / Delirium* picked up the gong. Recent work by Whyte and Martin MacIntyre has been published in Italian, Welsh and Catalan translation; Rody Gorman's *Sweeney* seems himself writing his work between multiple languages (Scottish Gaelic included).

As with the rest of the Gaelic world, there is an institutional infrastructure in place too. The Gaelic Books Council and the Scottish Book Trust support a Gaelic New Writer award every year. The *Ùr-Sgeul* scheme saw an explosion in new fiction (novels and short stories) for the ten years it ran (with *Gormshuil an Rìgh* being one of the books it published), and although that scheme has ended other publishers, such as Luath Press in Edinburgh, have helped continue the momentum of Clàr and Acair before them.

It is a book published by Luath that is sitting under *Gormshuil an Rìgh* on my desk, waiting its turn. *Far na Slighe* by Shelagh Chaimbeul is part of the nascent thread of Gaelic crime novels (murder still sells more than sex, in Gaelic too). This is a novel and writer that have both had a lot of support. Chaimbeul was a New Writer Award winner in 2022; another manuscript of hers won best manuscript for children or young people at the 2023 Gaelic Book Awards (themselves only established in 2010); she also learnt Gaelic as an adult, and worked for some years at the Gaelic Books Council. This is all to the good. In the Gaelic world we are now in a position where things happen less organically, where it is very unlikely a generation of writers on the north tip of Lewis will emerge together without encouragement (other than their own egging on, competition and rivalry); people from all communities and backgrounds need to be fostered, supported, and – crucially – have their work read and talked about (*mea culpa maxima mea culpa* for those sins of omission).

And so to *Far na Slighe*. "Off the Path" it could be translated. From the blurb it is a Gaelic "I have no idea what you did 20 summers' ago": a bracelet found 20 years ago on the coastal path near St Andrews could be crucial to a murder being discussed in a new "true crime" documentary series online. Why won't the three teenagers who were with Amy (our main character) talk to her about it? Why is this in Gaelic when St Andrews had so little of the language 20 years ago or, as I know well, now? Who cares! Murder, historical guilt, pulp, all in Gaelic. A different way of dealing with the past, a different meeting of forms of storytelling, but storytelling nonetheless: I can't wait.

Peter Mackay was born in the Isle of Lewis in 1979. He has an MLitt from University of Glasgow and a PhD from Trinity College Dublin. His poetry pamphlets and collections are From Another Island *(Clutag 2010),* Gu Leòr / Galore *(Acair, 2015) and* Nàdur De / Some Kind of *(Acair, 2021). He has co-edited poetry anthologies:* An Leabhar Liath *(Luath, 2016),* 100 Dàn as Fheàrr Leinn *(Luath, 2020), and* The Golden Treasury of Scottish Verse *(Canongate, 2021). He is Senior Lecturer in Literature at the School of English at University of St Andrews. He lives in Edinburgh.*

THE CRITICAL STATE OF SCOTTISH BOOK REVIEWING

Rosemary Goring

Erosions of space.

"If the printing of such trash as this be not felt as an insult on the public taste, we are afraid it cannot be insulted." So wrote Francis Jeffrey, editor of *The Edinburgh Review*, on the publication of William Wordsworth's *Poems, in Two Volumes* in 1807. Nor was he any more impressed by the poet's epic "The Excursion" in 1814, beginning his famous tirade: "This will never do."

The derogatory tone of that assessment still has the power to make you wince, even though Wordsworth has long since won the argument. When Jeffrey meted out similar punishment to Byron's collected juvenilia, *Hours of Idleness*, the poet's riposte was the hard-hitting satire *English Bards and Scotch Reviewers*, written in heroic couplets. How often does a crushing put-down inspire such a glittering retort? In my experience, a letter of complaint to the editor or an aggrieved email is the more usual blowback, after which the reviewer is consigned to social Siberia for the rest of their – the writer's – career.

The Edinburgh Review, which began under Jeffrey's editorship in 1802, quickly became the preeminent critical journal in the English-speaking world, setting a standard for reviewing of literature – alongside discussions of science and politics – that few publications could match.

Despite Jeffrey's prejudice against the fashionable romantic sensibility in poetry and fiction, the journal was epitomised by Enlightenment values: the desire fearlessly to question and evaluate matters of philosophy, science, religion, politics, literature and art. Yet, as its editor's blindness to Wordsworth's and Byron's talent shows, its purpose was not to lay down the law as if on tablets of granite, but to act as a vehicle for lively and rigorous critiques, be it of a political faction or a poet. The aim was to set people talking and arguing. In achieving this, it turned considered reviews into a unique art form.

Jeffrey and his anonymous, well-paid team of writers, many of whom were famous authors, established Scotland as the fulcrum of literary criticism. Their sometimes-pitiless pens earned the country's reviewers a reputation for unsentimental, well-informed and fearsome analysis, a distinction which lasted well into our own times. Sadly, however, such reviewing is in rapid decline.

Since Jeffrey's era, and until recently, Scotland nurtured a raft of influential literary journals and magazines, some state-sponsored, others independent; some high-profile, others niche but well-regarded. The health of literary criticism could be seen in the prominence given to books in national newspapers, which prided themselves on the breadth and calibre of their review pages. A former editor of *The Herald* (previously the *Glasgow Herald*), where for many years I was literary editor, told me that he could judge the quality and seriousness of a paper by the tone of its books pages. For him, they were the litmus test.

Today, review pages have been superseded by opinion columns, many drawing more on emotion than rational argument. Newspapers once viewed themselves as bulwarks of culture, but that is no longer the case, since the funds to maintain these pages have all but evaporated. As a result, space devoted to book reviews, as well as that for music, theatre, film, dance and art, is shrinking as fast as the polar ice cap.

At one point a few years ago I was running the books pages of three newspapers simultaneously: *The Herald*, the *Sunday Herald* and the *National*, which came into being following the Independence referendum in 2014. By then the heyday of books pages was already past. Nevertheless, between them these titles could offer an overview of the literary scene that was not derisory.

Long before the *National* was added to my remit, I saw the number of pages under my watch fluctuate like the weight of a yo-yo dieter. They would shrink or expand depending on the newspapers' fortunes or the priorities of their increasingly short-lived editors. At their peak, I was running 12 pages between *The Herald* and *Sunday Herald*. The same elasticity typified other serious Scottish newspapers, such as *The Scotsman* and *Scotland on Sunday*. Nor has this been an issue that merely afflicts publications north of the border. What has been going on here is replicated across the UK, albeit less starkly. Perhaps it feels particularly acute in Scotland, not just because the trend is more marked, but because this is where the book review was, in effect, invented.

As literary editor, I was able to track the diminishing importance of books in the media by the size of the book cupboard where my weekly intake of 200-plus books had to be stored and sorted. I started with a windowless room large enough for an emperor-size bed, and ended with a handful of shelves in a closet shared with the fashion editor and rails of designer clothes awaiting models and photoshoots. The daily sack loads of parcels flooded the room as if washed in by the tide, and finding a home for those books that could not be reviewed was a necessary and urgent chore, without which it would quickly have become impossible to open the door.

It's hard to credit that there was a time, considerably before my day, when the person doing my job at *The Herald* had an office of his own, complete with drinks cabinet. He was asked to write one review a month, but only if he felt like it. Not much before then, the paper's deputy editor, George Macdonald Fraser, would fill the time after the first edition went to press by tinkering on his novels. Nor was he alone.

Until relatively recently, the importance of literature was seen as a civilising force, and a marker of a paper's sophistication. Today, the post of newspaper literary editor is going the way of snuff-taking, as is the perceived value of dispassionate criticism. Given the parlous economics of the newspaper realm, literary criticism is an increasingly expendable luxury. Those who doggedly protect what few pages they have are clinging on by their fingertips.

Publishers in part share the blame for their disappearance. For many years, there was a sense of entitlement in some of the larger London publishing houses, who expected their books to be reviewed and their authors interviewed, yet would not consider placing adverts that would help safeguard the future of these pages.

The erosion of space is, of course, not a new phenomenon. It has been a problem for many years now. In 2004, the publishers Derek Roger of Argyll Books and Hugh Andrew of Birlinn, along with my journalist husband Alan Taylor, founded the quarterly journal, the *Scottish Review of Books*, which took as its model the *London Review of Books*. Disheartened by the Lilliputian coverage in papers and magazines, they hoped the *SRB* would meet the need for long-form, critical analysis, where properly remunerated reviewers were given the opportunity expansively to dissect books and address a range of subjects, political as well as cultural.

Alongside reviews of poetry, fiction and non-fiction, as well as author interviews, there were essays on subjects such as the growing tension in the South China Sea, the size of footballs in the run-up to the World Cup, and the influence of the independence movement on the country's writers. Edited, unpaid, from our kitchen table, it reached an estimated 300,000-plus readers a year, thanks to being distributed free with the *Herald*, and given away in libraries, museums, schools and book festivals, with advertising and subscriptions helping to pay towards its costs.

With an annual grant, initially from the Scottish Arts Council, which morphed into Creative Scotland, it thrived for 15 years. Then, in 2019, funding was withdrawn. When Alan and one of *SRB*'s directors met Creative Scotland to ask what had prompted this decision, they were told that, if they liked, they could reapply at the next round of fund applications and ask for more money to turn it into a bigger journal. The position of editor, of course, would remain unpaid.

They did not acknowledge that ceasing publication in the meantime would be its death knell. Nor could Alan and all those who worked for nothing behind the scenes take on a heavier workload without remuneration. In 2018, the estimated value of this unpaid labour was £45,500. On the news of its funding being withdrawn, the novelist James Robertson told *The Times* that "It's almost as if somebody at Creative Scotland has said, 'This has been going on too long!' *SRB*'s longevity is a major reason why it should not be killed off, especially as in the intervening years the space for serious literary reviewing in other places has drastically diminished."

Its demise was an indication that Creative Scotland did not care about literary journalism. Since then, no alternative magazine has sprung up to replace it, nor, so far as I am aware, been encouraged to do so. As a result, in subsequent years the reviewing landscape has grown even bleaker. The fear is that one day soon it might become tundra.

Not all is hopeless. Newspapers continue to review books and run book-related features, to a greater or lesser degree. In this respect the *Sunday Post* has shown its hitherto dormant cultural credentials. There is, too, a number of committed literary magazines, among them *Gutter*, *Dark Horse* and *Northwards Now*, all supported by Creative Scotland. Their circulation is small, as are the fees they offer contributors. And, although they include very short reviews, these are not their main focus.

Several factors are at work in this changing culture of criticism, not all of them attributable solely to the decline of literary journalism. The environment in which reviewing used to flourish has changed significantly in the past 20 years. Where once publishers had to accept hard-hitting reviews – sometimes they actually helped sell a book – now they prefer blander stuff that won't dent the author's reputation or feelings. Far better for the book's success are online puffs by fans (or family and friends), comments such as "I

<3 this!" and five-star ratings instantly boosting sales. No matter that online reviews can equally be ignorant, malevolent and anonymous, unfiltered by any editor's hand. In this unmoderated arena, books are treated like gladiators in the arena, a raised or lowered thumb determining their fate. At the same time, an author's talent for self-promotion can make the difference between eking out a living and fading unnoticed from the shelves.

None of this would be a problem if traditional reviewing – well-edited pieces by informed, experienced reviewers – remained in good health. Despite the sometimes savage nature of social media, the world of books is typified by a prevailing mood of back-slapping and hype rather than reasoned, well-written evaluation. The appetite for measured appraisals has faded, to be replaced with the fast food equivalent. In part, I suspect, it's to do with powers of concentration, and reluctance to spend time reading an essay. We're growing so used to at-a-glance ratings, whether on TripAdvisor or Netflix, it seems we are no longer interested in following an in-depth critique, with its nuanced and carefully calibrated praise or reservations.

We're often told we get the politicians we deserve. If that's true, then the same applies to books. The decline of thoughtful, well-informed assessments goes hand in hand with the loss of thoughtful, well-informed readers. This tightening circle creates an escalating downward spiral, producing a proliferation of formulaic fiction and unadventurous, copy-cat publishing that is designed to create bestsellers rather than discover writing so original it startles, provokes or beguiles.

For this shift of emphasis, creative writing courses are partly culpable. In many universities and colleges, what tutors secretly hope to find is not the new Henry James, but the next J. K. Rowling. What a boost that would be to their credibility, popularity and funding. Meanwhile, tutors on courses where quality and individuality are still prized know that only a few of their students have a chance of being published, and even fewer of making a career from their writing.

Criticism, which in some quarters is viewed as an expression of elitism, is falling foul of a mindset, within the arts, in which making value judgements is seen as inherently unacceptable and unfair. What right has anyone to pontificate on another's work?

Well, surely as much right as any writer to have a book published. Such suspicion is baffling, especially since in almost every other line of work there are analysts and experts whose role it is to monitor and report on standards, be it the performance of a premier league club or a health board.

More worrying, at least from my perspective, is the idea that an essay-length review is becoming a rarity. Part of the pleasure of reading such reviews is getting a balanced, knowledgeable take on a particular book or subject. When it comes to fiction and poetry especially, we all recognise there is no such thing as perfection. Across history, only a handful will ever come close to achieving this. But nobody expects perfection from creative writers. How unlike real life and our understanding of the world that would be.

Instead, the critical capacities brought to bear on any work of art are in themselves an exemplar of how we approach life: putting the subject in context, searching for its meaning, and questioning the way it has been put together, and how effectively. In my experience, the analysis can be as fascinating as the work under review. Equally often, it inspires the reader to approach a book they would not otherwise have considered. Nor does the review have to be wholly positive. Cavils and doubts sometimes make the work all the more intriguing.

I recently read a long essay by the American novelist Brandon Taylor in a back issue of the *London Review of Books*, about Émile Zola's 20-volume cycle, *Les Rougon-Macquart*. It was riveting, especially because of Taylor's honesty about the failings as well as the brilliance of individual works. For those keen to read Zola for themselves, he selected four titles as outstanding, recognising that: "You will probably never read all twenty of *Les Rougon-Macquart*. I know that. You know that. Let us accept this truth between us."

But even acknowledging that probability, my understanding of Zola, and what he was trying to achieve, has been immeasurably expanded. The piece itself was such an enjoyable read – an aspect of good book reviewing that is frequently overlooked – that I have added Taylor's own novels to my wishlist.

In Scotland especially, but also elsewhere, the chances of writers getting a published review are now so slim that publishers have to dampen their hopes before publication. Every day I receive emails from publishers and authors desperate for a notice. Unless they are high-profile, what a writer can realistically expect upon publication is a handful of online reviews at best. Today, being invited to appear at a book festival is almost essential if a writer's work is to reach the public eye. Yet, in the same way that most publishers ration how many literary novels and poetry collections they publish, since their sales are low, the literary content of book festivals wanes by the year. People flock to hear powerless politicians, moonlighting celebrities and attention-craving TV personalities, but writers who have laboured for years on their novels and poems go unnoticed. The cruel economics of the book trade consign those who should be at its beating heart into the cold.

It is hard to look at the future of the literary scene with anything approaching optimism. Despite the sense of community among writers, and a slew of state-sponsored initiatives intended to promote their work, it is increasingly obvious that crowd-pleasing books are preferred to those that take risks and stretch what fiction or poetry, or indeed non-fiction can do.

In this scenario, there seems less need than ever for literary critics. Yet without them, readers will be left adrift in a sea of books with no clue where north lies. What we need in these judgemental yet strangely unanalytical times is not so much a renaissance as a re-enlightenment.

Rosemary Goring was born near Dunbar in 1962, and studied history at the University of St Andrews. A journalist and editor, who regularly abridges fiction and non-fiction for BBC Radio Four, she was the Literary Editor of Scotland on Sunday, The Herald, *and the* Sunday Herald. *She has written several books, among them* After Flodden *(Polygon, 2013) and* Dacre's War *(Polygon, 2015), as well as editing the anthologies* Scotland: The Autobiography *(Penguin, 2014) and* Scotland: Her Story *(Birlinn, 2018). Her most recent work is* Exile: The Captive Years of Mary, Queen of Scots *(Birlinn, 2022). She lives in the Scottish Borders, where her novels are set.*

D'OÙ VENONS-NOUS / QUE SOMMES-NOUS / OÙ ALLONS-NOUS

―

Don Paterson

Shaking it out.

Remember *The Vow*? Most of us have tried to forget it. This was Westminster's Hail Mary as polling day approached in the 2014 referendum; a vote that Yessers – people tend to forget this part too – initially had no real expectation of winning, until an inspirationally positive campaign saw the polls draw neck-and-neck. Then Lo! There it was, splashed across the *Daily Record*: a fancy-font promise from Westminster party leaders that if Scotland voted to stay within the UK, we would enjoy new devolved powers. There was some other waffle about defence and opportunities and having an equal share in the UK's prosperity. But the message was clear enough. We would be *listened to*.

Aye, right. The emptiness of the promise was exposed the day after the vote; our own collapse of imagination, will and confidence took years, but the two are related. The full tortuous story will stand as a kind of cautionary tale for all small nations seeking their independence. My original title was "Notes upon Cancelling my SNP Membership", but Gauguin's famous title will lend it a little more allegorical drama. (It will also leave a vague stink of orientalism hanging over this essay; I hope a few readers will understand why.) The occasion may be local, but the conclusions are miserably broad. But if we're to figure out who we now are and where the hell we're going, there should be some mundane rehearsal of how we got here.

A couple of years before the referendum, I recall thinking that Westminster was smart to let the rebranding of the Scottish Executive as "the Scottish Government" pass with an indulgent wink. Even though it didn't have the fiscal independence of a real national government, Holyrood could now be blamed for the consequences of any Westminster-generated policy disaster that happened to wash up in Scotland. People blame their governments for everything. But the bold adoption of ScotGov was also a sign of a growing appetite for independence. The SNP had won a simple majority in Holyrood. This was supposed to be impossible: our part-PR D'Hondt-method electoral system was designed to force coalition. (It is also designed not to be fair, but to appear fair: how clever to ask Scotland to hold itself to higher standards of electoral democracy while it remained nested within the rotten old Westminster FPTP system, with all its wasted votes, safe-seatery, bumps to the Lords and gerrymandered fix.) A year after the referendum, in the Westminster elections, the ones that *really* mattered, the SNP won 56 out of 59 seats. A UK-wide party which had enjoyed the same popularity would have won 617 out of 650. This left them with what any other non-insane part of Western Europe would've acknowledged as an overwhelming democratic mandate.

And yet, it swiftly transpired, no will or courage to act upon it. Now was the moment to force the issue, to try *something*; to declare independence based on electoral mandate, then argue for its legitimacy under the UN charter; to unilaterally ignore the Reserved Matter rules, and dare Westminster to mothball Holyrood; to withdraw SNP MPs in protest, in acknowledgement of the impossibility of ever forcing a second referendum within the Westminster system; to call an unofficial second referendum without a section 30 order ... None were great plans, true, and all carried huge risks. But now was the time to do *something*. (Our wisest heid, Neal Ascherson, addresses some of these points herein.)

At this point, the old lullaby of "too wee, too poor and too stupid" seemed to whisper again in our ears. Covid, admittedly, meant that for a year or two the literal health of the nation had to be placed above that of its body politic. But for all many of us admired Sturgeon's humane and reassuring performances at the daily Covid briefing, we suspected she was also deeply relieved to be off the hook. As the crisis abated, the old fear made itself known. After its new policy of asking Westminster really, *really* nicely failed, our principal independence party declared that we required not just an electoral mandate to call a second vote, but a 60% pro-independence *opinion poll*. From a Unionist, such an absurd call would make perfect sense; but for the SNP to set this as the benchmark for "the settled will of the Scottish people" looked exactly like the terrified procrastination it was.

Nor, one belatedly realised, was this commitment to total stasis merely the consequence of the fear of acting without the permission of our Westminster overlords. Stuart Campbell, the notorious, hugely influential pro-independence gadfly better known as Wings over Scotland (SNP MSPs are barred from following him; all do), began to expose the extent to which the status quo suited the SNP and its finances. Tales of careerist Westminster "troughers" and reports of Sturgeon locking herself in a steel bubble full of parrots and mirrors became harder to refute. The SNP's numerical majority in Holyrood was, of course, unsustainable, and it was soon forced into coalition with – and soon, ideological capture by – the Scottish Greens, a tiny pro-independence minority party with no constituency seats. Their eccentric and ill-conceived policy obsessions, many warned, would not survive a moment's contact with proper media scrutiny, let alone the electorate. But they, too, served an unconscious purpose for the SNP: allowing the culture and gender wars to consume so much political energy and airtime was an act of such colossal, self-defeating idiocy, it began to look like self-defeat was the point. Then, finally understanding that the party was bleeding support from the very voters it was formed to represent, Sturgeon declared that a simple Westminster majority would represent a *de facto* referendum. The desperation of that move – "de facto" is apparently Latin for "obviously not a" – need not be analysed here. The boat had been missed. There was no diem to carpe. Following one of the most badly timed political resignations in recent history, a dubiously shooed-in Sturgeon understudy, Humza Yusef, briefly doubled down on her folly before he, too, was destroyed by the Scottish Green alliance.

In the meantime, self-loathing had begun to eat away at our sense of ourselves. As with an individual, a country's sense of coherent identity is bound up in the strength of its public representation. Our many Unionists – half the country – had none in Westminster, which was dispiriting enough; but there was apparently nothing Indy supporters could do to advance their own cause either. "National pride" was being hollowed out by the very folk we'd voted in to bolster it. It increasingly seemed to me that Creative Scotland, and the smaller arts and literature organisations it supports, were dealing with the crisis in Scottish identity via a projected obsession with identity politics. "We don't know who we are, so you tell us who you are. Oh – and make it interesting." Identitarianism encourages people to simplify themselves, which is one reason it will always be a favoured tool of the state. It generates tribal division, and – consciously or not – works as a strategy of divide-and-rule which leaves the real power in the hands of the bureaucratic overseers. These divisions soon began to undermine the "civic and joyous" come-all-ye universalism the independence movement had recently aspired to. The sector employs many talented and conscientious individuals, and funds much good art; but the misplaced sense of self-importance that tends to dog the world of arts administration had led it to forget that its job was the nurturing and promotion of Scottish excellence and talent, not the defence of the culture's ideological purity. Then again, these institutions are always downstream of legislative culture; the same disconnect had happened via Blairite, corporate-speak neo-managerialism 20 years before.

As for that culture, we will spend years pop-psychoanalysing what the hell went wrong. Often it seemed political capital was spent and exhausted in controversial and marginal causes as a neurotic proxy for the one big one the SNP had, suddenly, no inclination or courage to tackle. Either way, the larger matters with which the general population was taken up – health, transport, education, sex equality, immigration, poverty, regional equality, sexual violence, drug addiction – went inadequately addressed, often – or at least so it appeared to the public – in favour of the SNP's increasingly cosmetic, proxy or marginal preoccupations. Elsewhere, the inherent flaws in popular SNP policies started to make themselves known. The SNP's populist insistence that Scots must be supplied free university education, alas, came without the wherewithal to fund it. This led to the mere appearance of its availability. Universities cannot subsidise the policy without heavy reliance on fees from international students, meaning some are obliged to cap Scottish places. At some universities, this means that Scottish students must meet higher bars for entry; ludicrously, Scottish applicants are at the same time used to fulfil admission targets for lower socioeconomic groups. Result: discrimination against the Scottish *middle* class, and working-class Scots sometimes finding themselves the *only* Scots in their entire student cohort, just in case they didn't already feel self-conscious enough. (The class- and xenophobic shaming of these students – particularly within a certain leading university *in our own country* – is now routinely reported.)

Elsewhere, The Cringe was back, and this time it's got a gym membership. Many friends have commented on how many institutions, university programmes and arts events have started to shed their distinctively Scottish identities like a bad smell. In the literary arts, we can still, mercifully, manage to make the occasional exception for writers working in the minority languages of Scots and Gaelic, and indeed we celebrated the appointment of a Gael to the post of Makar, Peter Mackay, who contributes an essay here. Elsewhere, however, a young artist with no more intersectional interest to their name than "Scottish" is plainly – can *anyone* seriously continue to argue this is not the case – at a blatant disadvantage. Their merely having grown up in the distinct cultures of West Kilbride, Papa Westray or Wester Hailes can no longer be leveraged in the only place on earth that could possibly care about it. Region and class (along with age, care-giving status, mental health, marital status, previous criminal record and a lot more besides) barely feature in our highly selective hierarchies of underrepresentation, suffering and disadvantage. Heigh ho; time to use what you've got, slap "lives with gluten intolerance" into your biography and pray it gains the sympathy of the awards panel. (I dearly wish I was making this example up.) But our regional identities, too, shape the distinct pattern of diversity that makes Scotland's unique. Besides, many regions suffer from terrible economic and cultural deprivation: folk are often more disadvantaged by their town of origin than by any other attribute. Why make so precious little of the fact? (The reason, of course, is that "region" and "class" are not name brands in the luxury belief system, which is to say that strain of lifestyle politics furthest divorced from the world of capital and labour.)

Artists are always somewhere making good work; they are not, however, always the artists promoted by the state. Music is harder to spoil, as its means of production instantly reveals a certain stratification of talent; besides, the ear is almost impossible to gaslight. Literature and the visual arts are in very different positions, and have proven far more vulnerable to the corrective ambitions of our gatekeepers. The result is not just that our institutions no longer defend the principle and further the cause of artistic excellence; they seem to have forgotten that their job was to showcase that excellence as *our own* distinct contribution to global culture.

You will also recall that The Vow was supposed to bring Scotland into the cultural and political heart of the nation. How did that shake out? In my own world of contemporary poetry, the two largest UK-wide awards, the Forward and TS Eliot prizes, have shortlisted twenty books over the last year. It's just as well the American-Iranian poet Marjorie Lotfi has long been a Scot, because without her, not a single writer from the entire Celtic fringe would have featured. (Then again, neither did a single UK white male, a mere 37% of the population.) There is no devolved-nation member on the board of the Royal Society of Literature. We've had years of this stuff; it now feels less like slight and more like trolling. We are at the heart of very little.

Such thoughtless deletions are mainly proof of a narrow, entirely ideological definition of "diverse" – one derived from recent US political history, and currently aligned not with a UK but a London demographic. But it also shows that we need Scottish institutions to promote talent drawn from our boring majority identities with exactly the same enthusiasm it shows for our minorities, for which it prefers to advocate. Edinburgh author Chitra Ramaswamy is quite correct in her assertion that "diversity is the realisation of quality". Or at least it should be: diversity leads to cross-pollination and creative ferment – and real talent is too thinly spared in the arts for any minority group to be ignored. But to achieve this, we need a definition of diversity that reflects the *entirety* of our real-world Scottish identity, of every defining aspect of our lives in Scotland: not just of ethnicity, sexual orientation and gender – but of class, sex, region, age, disability, faith, dialect, language.

Excuse all the italics, but this seems poorly understood: the *point* of nationalism is that one place gets to be different from another. Without cultural distinction, there *can* be no diversity. Diversity is a *justification* for nationalism. Small countries dominated by larger imperial or pseudo-imperial powers should fight to retain their distinctive cultural identity as an act of resistance to the monocultures they seek to impose. And yet our own gatekeepers continue to take their cultural lead from London – now not only deferred to as our real seat of government, but as a holy reservoir of liberal wisdom – and from America, for whom Scotland is rapidly becoming a little safe haven for an increasingly discredited politics of identity, whose cosiness with neoliberalism should alarm its followers. Scotland will be the last to get the memo, as usual.

But what else but a lack of national pride could explain, for example, our failure to arrest the infantile antics of Fossil Free Books, and their craven, entirely confected attack on three layers of soft underbelly – Scotland, book festivals, and one of the most ecologically *responsible* investors and major patrons of the arts, Baillie Gifford. Prominent among their "book worker" ringleaders were some overconfident, expensively educated English students, and several folk "currently living in Scotland", whose first major cultural intervention was to trash beautiful things that others had spent decades building. (At no point did the young authors involved bother to "follow the money" with regard to who sells their *own* books, or where the pension funds of their own publishers are invested.) Why did we not rally round our besieged festivals, and say "enough is enough"? I'm afraid one has to conclude that some recent arrivals clearly see their role as culturally corrective, much like the Italian dance-masters shipped to Edinburgh in the early 19th century to fix our rustic fiddle-playing. Our low-ebb confidence currently offers far too little resistance, especially, to some smug yanksplanation. In the light of what we will tactfully call "recent events over the pond", I might gently request that our newer American arrivals firstly consider a period of quiet reflection, and secondly, check their privilege: as members of the planet's leading cultural hegemon, it would behove them to cultivate a less American and Anglocentric understanding of the range and varieties of colonial, class and regional oppression.

Which brings us, almost exquisitely, to the campaign to erase David Hume from the building that until recently bore his name. Hume is generally regarded as the greatest philosopher of the modern age, and the most important figure in the Scottish Enlightenment, that critical era in the tradition of thought that brought us everything from modern science to the human rights movement. He was a critical influence on Kant, Mill and Darwin; Einstein credited Hume with inspiring the approach which led to the general principle of relativity. While he was alive, Hume's debunking of religion and social prejudice meant he never gained the institutional status he deserved. He argued vehemently and at length against the idea that the character and potential of humans is determined by race. David Hume might be the Scot we should be most proud of. He also penned a single footnote which was entirely typical of the ignorant racism of the age. It is so internally contradictory and out-of-step with his general view that some scholars believe it to be satirical; but no, it's a stinker. Nonetheless, the idea that Hume has *nothing* to offer in the way of mitigation, excuse and compensatory virtue is beyond insane. The international student behind the successful petition candidly admitted she knew nothing of the most significant intellectual oeuvre ever produced by the city which had offered her an academic home, and suggested that his tower be renamed after Julius Nyerere, as several scholarships already are. Nyerere was an important leader and thinker – one with, as an Edinburgh University alumnus, considerable debts to Hume. He also believed homosexuality to be un-African, and was the dictatorial leader of a one-party state who imprisoned its political opponents. But hey, at least he wasn't Scottish. (The student later withdrew this suggestion with a priceless "It has been brought to my attention", after a completing a little of that activity indispensable to the naming of public buildings, "further research".)

In kowtowing to this ignorant and childish demand, the university did grave damage to Scotland's intellectual integrity. Presumably fearful of offending the wealthy international student body who now cough up the fees the SNP have left it chasing – it offered instead something like a national apology. Most of us agreed that Scotland's postcolonial reckoning was long overdue, but (as Amanda Thomson explains in her essay here) the reckoning is also distinctly *ours*: complex, local, contextual and nuanced. Despite what you might think, guys: we have this one.

But the truth is, all you postgraduate lifestylers, all you gap-year activists, all you good folks "currently living in": I love you, really. We need you to stay. We desperately need the immigration. We need your expertise, labour, taxes and children. We have much to offer in return, besides a home in the most beautiful country on earth. I would have only a few things to request of every "New Scot" – whether student, academic, artist, doctor, joiner or asylum seeker. Lord knows, you don't have to support Scottish independence. All I'd ask is that you notice you are in a place called Scotland, with its own history, culture and political balance; that you care about the present and the future of that country; that you are prepared to invest in its culture and society, rather than set yourself on destroying or denigrating it; and that you contribute to as well as draw on public funds. We desperately want you to be proud of this place, and make the place your own. That's all. As soon as you declare it so, you will find out that the Scots will fight for you exactly as we would our own; because that is how they now regard you.

However it's perhaps time to admit that our perennial call to "work as if you lived in the early days of a better nation" has become something of an empty shibboleth. The petty, tribal, prescriptive, censorious, identity-obsessed and philistine culture the SNP have created has left many older centrist heids reluctant to speak up over matters of simple common sense and public concern, conceding many of them not just to the right (with whom they are now occasionally driven to make common cause), but – far more dangerously – to the self-declared racists, sexists, homophobes and fascists who should represent our common enemy. The SNP are also, in their current incarnation, poor stewards of the independence dream. As we enter a pre-war era of economic uncertainty and shifting alliances, rediscovering it will be a far more sober and adult task than we have previously had to face. We first must decide what it is we mean by "better nation". It will have to be one with considerably more courage, genuine inclusivity and stomach for honest and civil debate than we currently demonstrate. It will require us to tackle the kinds of broad disadvantage that animate the electorate, as well as those narrow causes which excite our political and institutional leaders. It will require an Enlightenment-style revival of an artistic and intellectual meritocracy, one which can actively connect and draw on the talents of an increasingly diverse but distinctively Scottish society. It may also require a properly articulated constitution. For one thing, a great many older Scots – having seen quite enough in the way of sectarian hatred and violence to last us a lifetime – would far prefer that the First Minister be attended on by neither minister, priest nor imam while resident in Bute House.

We may have to bring along our Unionist friends by considering less radical, federal solutions on the longer road to full independence. The movement has been derailed by many other things besides identity politics: cowardice, personality cult, unwise alliances, middle-management overreach, a bureaucratic, form-obsessed culture of mutual distrust, self-imposed busywork, Holyrood bubbles and Westminster troughers. It will be righted on its tracks as soon as we can remember that we can also build movements without the politicians and institutions that currently divide us through increasingly morbid and inward-looking agendas. Until they can be trusted to represent us again, it may be time for artists to wean themselves off institutional support, at least where they can, through the direct engagement of audiences, readers and students that the digital age offers, and through private sponsorship and investment. It is certainly time to decouple the independence movement from the party who do not, at present, serve its interests well.

More than anything else, we should see our increasing diverse population – first and foremost – as an opportunity to celebrate all we have in *common*, without diminishing the enriching possibilities of our differences. We are all Jock Tamson's bairns, and – Yesser or Yoon – patriotism should be nothing more than the means by which we extend our feeling of family to the limits of our borders, and through consciously exercising that faculty, the rest of humanity too.

See biographical note on p 15.

ALL THE RAGE: REFLECTIONS ON A FRACTIOUS DECADE FOR LIVE POETRY IN SCOTLAND

Jenny Lindsay

Between the analogue and the digital.

In August 2014, Colin Waters, then editor of small poetry imprint Vagabond Voices and the Communications Manager of the Scottish Poetry Library, was making the final touches to his foreword to a new anthology of Scottish poetry. Titled *Be The First To Like This*, the collection aimed to showcase the spectrum of young or new voices emerging from the plethora of live poetry events across Scotland, including those cutting their teeth at the cabaret series Rally & Broad, which I ran with fellow poet Rachel McCrum, shortly to become the first BBC Radio Scotland Poet in Residence. That position was advertised as seeking, very specifically, a poet with a performance or "spoken word" background.

Waters was writing his foreword during a period of enormous enthusiasm for such events. These included the match-funded (via ticket-sales and Creative Scotland funding) and carefully curated Rally & Broad events where new voices from both the performance and literary worlds would be showcased alongside Makars and well-known faces from other art forms. Also all the rage at the time was Michael Pedersen and Kevin Williamson's "Neu! Reekie!" which enjoyed spectacular audiences and unprecedented funding, and regularly featured famous names from the worlds of music and literature. These bigger, funded events were supported – and benefitted from – a thriving grassroots network of smaller events that offered the opportunity for connection and informal mentoring via open mics with guest performers, events which were regularly scouted by those of us looking out for exciting new poets to offer a bigger stage. Whatever one's poetic inclinations – from the slam-style of youthful North-American-inspired polemics to the more literary (or some combination of the two) – there was a core event an audience member could support. There was a very keenly felt sense of being part of a "scene".

This period, 2010 – 2014, was a real turning point for my own career as a poet and programmer, but also for performance poetry and live poetry events generally. Loud Poets, a rotating collective of very young and confident twenty-somethings operating mainly via the university networks – so unashamedly (at the time) focused on polished performances, all poets were banned from performing other than from memory. They bolshily worked their way into the scene, bridging a gap between generations, while ruffling many feathers in the process. My art form – one I'd steadfastly plugged away at since my early twenties, often as the sole twenty-something in the room – no longer felt as "niche" as it once had.

Waters says he was moved to create the anthology while he reflected on the contrast between the cultural mood in Scotland in his teenage years, a time of Scottish cultural cringe, with the undeniable cultural confidence the country had recovered by 2014 in the run-up to the Scottish independence referendum. "When Scots are confronted with a major political choice," he wrote, "they talk and argue about it. And poetry is one of the ways in which our nation conducts that debate." Crucially, he added that he was not suggesting that poetry was being used as a political weapon, nor that the live poetry scene was urging its audiences into a fractious war of words. Instead, he suggested, what the rising popularity and undeniable success of the live poetry scene showed was "a vote of confidence in Scotland as a place of interest and worth." Would it last, he wondered? Might there be a post-referendum slump, as there was after the failure of the first devolution referendum of his teens? He was cautiously optimistic. Weren't we all.

As I reflect on the last decade in Scottish live poetry, I am struck that, just as Waters was in 2014, I cannot separate my views on the health of the art form from my views about the health of our democracy. Furthermore, this is largely due to the same intertwining factors: how we, as poets, as citizens, sit in judgement of each other; and how we, as poets, as citizens, conduct important cultural and political debates.

The title *Be The First To Like This* was chosen in 2014, Waters said, to reflect that the poets in the collection were coming of age in a new, exciting era, where social media offered new ways to network and build audiences. It is true to say that the invention of YouTube and other means of disseminating live poetry could be said to have been a net positive, in terms of things like "engagement", "likes" and "shares", and where discussion about the themes of one's work could find an eager, communicative audience. Poet Hollie McNish, who had been a seasoned poet and performer for some time, had, in 2014, recently gone "viral" with an off-the-cuff, roughly edited upload of one of her poems for use in a workshop; with an unexpected and burgeoning new audience, she soon found she was able to become a full-time writer. Others looked on with both admiration and envy, and over the years it has become routine for younger poets to upload their poems to similar forums, with "going viral" a core aim.

Outside of the performance world – and also in 2014 – young Canadian poet Rupi Kaur had used Instagram to start building a following that, at the time of writing, stands at 4.4 million. Her 2014 debut collection *Milk and Honey* sold over 2 million copies. Such a thing in *poetry* was fairly unprecedented. As with McNish, such popularity and financial success brought intense scrutiny. Though McNish had a prior audience, and achieved literary acclaim as well as popularity, and though Kaur's success was built via a focus on visual imagery and "branding" rather than, say, via traditional modes of publishing, led to some harsh words from many regarding their literary merit. Just in the way many had closely followed McNish's journey, other poets have attempted to replicate Kaur's relatively unique career trajectory. My eyebrow raised around 2015 when I saw a young, up-and-coming "spoken word" poet advertise that she was running a workshop focused on how to create an online "brand" out of oneself in the pursuit of a poetry career. Aged thirty-three, then, I didn't feel particularly old, but I did feel I was between the analogue and the digital ways of doing things.

I have watched these new trends from the position of someone solely focused on supporting a healthy *live* scene for both performance and literary poets, with a possibly curmudgeonly attitude towards the alleged benefits of posting sometimes unpolished or unfinished online "content" to the world. Additionally, while it would be odd to ignore a new and relatively cheap way to advertise live events, I am keenly aware that it takes a super-confidence not all of us have to film, "brand" and market *ourselves*. An over-emphasis on such a trait in an art-form that has traditionally attracted the reclusive and shy would seem counter-productive, and likely to miss a great deal of excellent literary poetry, as well as leave behind those comfortable performing only in a live setting, rather than broadcasting to the entire world.

Something that I and other performance poets had long been concerned about – before social media even took off – was how to gain proper feedback and critique as a performance poet when there was a lack of proper review, when literary critics appeared to be on a spectrum between dismissive and snooty, when theatre critics might enthuse about the performance and narrative but fail to notice the poetry, and where "spoken word" poets had long been an accused of being all performance and no substance. I had always felt it pointless to demand I be reviewed as one would a literary poet. During the editorial process for *Be The First To Like This*, there were only three of my poems I felt might work as well on the page as they did in performance. Ordinarily, my creations would push the five-minute mark – not exactly conducive to their inclusion in what was, at the end of the day, a print anthology. While others around me dropped the "performance" descriptor from their biographies, by 2014, which marked roughly fourteen years of navigating this strange tightrope between poetry, performance, storytelling, theatrics, I clung to it for this reason.

"If it doesn't exist, create it!"

This was my mantra back in the early noughties as a young poet/ event programmer, as I worked to build the kind of opportunities for performance poets enjoyed by our more literary siblings. Performance poetry, now re-branded by most as "spoken word" (and, by others, simply "poetry") was always, for me, a very different art-form from literary poetry, with more in common with storytelling and narrative comedy. Though they wrote *entirely* for a live audience, when I was starting out in this scene in my twenties it was not common for performance poets to pursue publishing deals or to appear at literary festivals. Club nights and music gigs, yes. The Author's Yurt? Hardly.

There was a great deal of laughter from certain quarters about performance poetry and its poets, a then motley bunch of largely self-taught performers who had found the art form via various routes, none of which included studying creative writing at university. But never mind the scornful, we reasoned – we wrote for audiences, not for snooty poets and writers. And the "liveness" was key. While many of us in the early noughties would self-publish pamphlets to sell after our performances as a way to improve our often-paltry fees, we were under no illusion that someone who hadn't actually *heard* those poems performed would be as moved (in whatever way we'd intended) by their reading them on the page, and alone.

Of course, we performance poets were rather popular with a diverse public – perhaps more so than some of our literary brethren, who were, for their part, far more popular than we were in the academy and with readers. Around 2006, publishers and literary festivals began to notice our popularity with live audiences, and we started to receive invitations to spaces we'd never been offered before. For some of us, it was now possible to do something most of us hadn't really considered: make a living from being a performance poet. There weren't many of us. But young poets, both performance and literary, soon started coming through the ranks who, having done well on their university courses, began to look enviously at what they assumed to be a natural trajectory: write some poems for your Literature Society, get on a few stages, put out a semi-viral film-poem, publish a pamphlet, and *voila!* A *career* as a poet can thus be made and, moreover, can be expected. The prevailing attitude might be summed up in one word: entitlement.

I have lost count of the number of times I have had to bite my tongue as a recent graduate from a Russell Group university bemoans the lack of career opportunities as a writer/performer, when they have written one collection, and have been doing live readings for about eighteen months or so. *The "career" is to keep writing and keep improving.* In the mix, too, is a rise in fractiousness over issues of identity in Scotland due to the government's legislative priorities, notably arguments over race and gender identity. Poets and writers have duked it out on the wild west of Twitter/X, with some poets having their work and their viewpoints judged not on their merit, but by the demographic categories their author/speaker belongs to. Depending on which those are, this might be a positive or a negative for any individual.

Far from what those of us who worked so hard to build routes of progression for budding verse-makers wanted – with an over-focus on "branding" and identity, and a serious shortage of proper scouts for both literary and performance poetry, genuinely good work is being overlooked in favour of those who can fulfil the non-artistic aims and objectives of literary organisations and quangos, who also live in terror of a social media pile-on. Over the ten years since the referendum and since *Be The First To Like This*, a perfect storm has been brewing.

Older, established writers and poets have tended to eschew such platforms as they have no need for them (and value their sanity), but that has meant that those of us stuck between the generations have had to contend with these forces with very little support. Where the expectation of a "career" meets financial precarity, social media, and a rise in a politics focused on identity; where poets and writers are encouraged to focus their craft on identity and branding rather than any pretence at universal themes; where cultural edicts demand the same priorities in our institutions too – the conditions are created for social media "houndings" or "cancellations" – even demands for no-platforming – of poets by fellow poets and writers, something that has become a focus of my own recent poetry and non-fiction.

There have been too many such incidents to recount fully, but by 2019, having witnessed several, I felt enormous disquiet as someone who prided herself on programming a true diversity of opinion in my event-series. This "scene" was rapidly becoming something censorious and unfamiliar. The year prior had seen a particularly egregious accusation spread amongst Scottish poets after an independent poetry reviewer wrote on his blog that the poet Toby Martinez de las Rivas, who had just been nominated for a Forward Prize, used his poetry to push a "nakedly fascist ideology". This spread, as smears do online, around the entire literary world before the truth could quite get its shoes on. Even to question whether Martinez could possibly be fairly accused of such was to risk denunciation, as many learnt to their cost. Nevertheless, Edinburgh poet Rob Mackenzie skilfully addressed the extraordinary fallout from the Martinez incident in *The Dark Horse* in 2019, noting that the persecution of Martinez was based in no small part, if not entirely, on a "highly dubious and probably rushed analysis of poems and an ignorance of the theological ideas that underpin much of the poetry." For his pains, Mackenzie was praised by many, while also being described by one young poet as a "crusty old white litbro".

This is no way to review the worth of a poem, nor a poet, nor a critic. But it has become routine to see poets dismissed not on the basis of their work, but on the nature of their politics; sometimes even on their *perceived* politics, assigned on the basis of their arbitrary demographic categories. Additionally, some literary critics, formerly known for their bite, seem wary of assessing the worth of a poem if it is written from a "marginalised" perspective. Again, this is of no use for a poet hoping for honest critique. Do poets still want this? I sometimes wonder if I am in the minority.

In early summer 2019, the formerly hopeful Colin Waters published a piece for the *Times Literary Supplement* in response to these new developments saying:

> The Scottish poetry community's culture wars will strike many reading as a punch-up in a phone box, but if a small, relatively contained poetry scene in which many involved know each other personally can't work out their differences, God knows how the country will.

I am quoted in this 2019 article as sharing similar concerns; that having tried "to moderate the wilder wings of Scottish poetry's clicktivist contingent," I had grave concerns over the rising censoriousness and fractiousness, which, it seemed to me then – and seems even more so now, a half-decade later – was taking the place of meaningful offline discussion or events; in fact it risked destroying the possibility of compassion across difference. Is this how we do poetry now? It is unrecognizable as any "scene" I would wish to be part of.

I am aware that this essay poses more questions than it offers answers. One day I would dearly hope to change my mind about the health of the Scottish live poetry scene, and, by extension, Scottish liberal democracy; to champion it once again as a place of true diversity of thought, of opinion, of style, and of substance. I still believe that if a healthy literary culture does not exist, we can create it. However, that must start with a full recognition of what we risk losing, and, what has already been lost.

Jenny Lindsay is one of Scotland's best-known spoken word performers, and her spoken word, theatre and music organisation, Flint and Pitch (est. 2016), was included in The List Magazine's *"Hot 100" for 2017. As an independent programmer and promoter of poetry, live literature and spoken word, Jenny has been credited with contributing to a thriving live poetry scene in Scotland. As one half of cult literary cabaret duo Rally & Broad (2012–16), she was described as "one of Scotland's finest cultural innovators"* (Gutter, 2015). *In December 2017 she was awarded the Creative Edinburgh Award for Leadership for her work in the spoken word sector. In 2024, Lindsay published* Hounded: Women, Harms and the Gender Wars *(Polity).*

LATE TO THE PARTY

Stuart Kelly

But back again.

I would have thought it no longer required reiterating, but literature is not like sunscreen, Tanquary No. 10 gin or a load-bearing wall. To talk about it in terms of strength is pointless; there are not even the equivalents of Scoville, Beaufort or Richter scale for literature. pH tests have more rigour. The question "what is the strength of contemporary Scottish literature?" is a minefield of unquantifiable propositions. Literature – indeed, the arts more generally – has long had an inferiority complex in terms of its academic status in contrast to the sciences and even the social sciences. The appropriate response to art is not a tick; neither as a sign of correctness nor as an item to have been "accounted for", "crossed off" or "done". It is plausible to view the close reading and "New Criticism" of I. A. Richard, Helen Vendler and Cleanth Brooks as a misguided scientism, as much as a certain recondite lexicon in post-structuralist criticism (which led it to being only too susceptible to such treatments as the Sokal hoax). This approach sought, in effect, to exorcise the very humanity from the humanities. Yet I take joy – joy is not too strong a word – in the precision or ingenuity of particular readings by critics as different as Lorna Sage, Jacques Derrida, Stanley Fish and Marina Warner.

To take an example: is J. K. Rowling evidence of the strength of contemporary Scottish literature? Is she Scottish? (What counts? Birth? Electoral register? Feeling that way that day?) Is it literature, with or without tweezer-like inverted commas? Do we judge it by column inches, sales, Goodreads stars? Is it contemporary: admittedly these are strange times but when the first Harry Potter novel came out there was no Wikipedia (2001), Facebook (2004), YouTube (2005), née-Twitter (2006), WhatsApp (2009), Instagram (2010) or TikTok (2016). There was no Scottish Parliament, and there have been eight UK prime ministers since. If one is looking for an unquestionable metric of the difference, and perhaps even the desuetude, of our days, in 1997 *there were only three Star Wars films.*

If the question is impossible to answer, the person to whom it is posed is now problematic as well. The question that was whispered has become a mandatory tocsin: *who are you to judge?* I shall be clear. I am a middle aged, astigmatic, middle-class man, educated at the local comprehensive and at Oxford, a Caucasian, non-practising heterosexual, and a Presbytery Elder in the Church of Scotland. One dear friend twits me as "Antediluvian Man", "the Relic" and "Casaubon". What gives you the right to judge?

I have written three books – *The Book of Lost Books: A Incomplete History of All the Books You'll Never Read*, *Scott-Land: The Man Who Invented A Nation* and *The Minister and the Murderer: A Book of Aftermaths* – but am known, if at all, as a reviewer. I don't know how many books I have read. I started in 1999 and became Literary Editor at *Scotland on Sunday* in 2005, and have written for a large number of other newspapers, magazines and journals. A very rough calculation would have a lower limit of 2,500 books, not including books I read for research, for pleasure or as an interviewer at public events (in one year, just before the pandemic, I did fifty-nine events). In addition I have judged the Man Booker Prize and the Granta Best of Young British Prize. That said, I accept that I might not be a slave as defined by Coleridge: "There are four kinds of readers. The first is like the hourglass; and their reading being as the sand, it runs in and runs out, and leaves not a vestige behind. A second is like the sponge, which imbibes everything, and returns it in nearly the same state, only a little dirtier. A third is like a jelly bag, allowing all that is pure to pass away, and retaining only the refuse and dregs. And the fourth is like the slaves in the diamond mines of Golconda, who, casting aside all that is worthless, retain only pure gems".

Of course, there is also "that's just your opinion". Well, I have never denied that. Nor would I claim my taste, such as it is, is somehow distinct from or unconnected to the facts of my personal circumstances. I would have different opinions if I had not read *The Seven Citadels* by Geraldine Harris at the age of eleven, or if I had made a different choice at the end of the first year at secondary school when my English teacher, Alec Beaton, said I could take home either *Great Expectations* or *Hamlet* for the summer holidays. (I chose *Hamlet*). There are some choices we make, and some situations that are bequeathed but we did not choose. I have tempered myself to my *Geworfenheit*, or "thrownness", to use the term from Heidegger. Or, to quote the Sermon on the Mount, "which of you by taking thought can add one cubit unto his stature?" "Here I stand", as Martin Luther said, "I can do no other". I do not think my accidental Scottishness, or any other characteristic, requires anything of me. In fact, reading in one newspaper that "if Stuart Kelly does not get some Scots on the Booker longlist, questions will be asked" left me more bemused than aggrieved.

To an extent, I missed out on the ebullience about Scottish literature. Being in Oxford during formative years, I first heard of *Trainspotting* when someone said to me that he wished he'd read it before the film meant everyone was talking about it. It meant nothing to me. Circumstance meant I was reading A. S. Byatt, Iris Murdoch, Nicholas Mosley, Iain Sinclair, Lawrence Norfolk, Donna Tartt and Muriel Spark, whom I only vaguely knew was Scottish; it was daring to read Poppy Z. Brite or Bret Easton Ellis, mandatory to read Grass and Márquez and Rushdie and DeLillo. The biggest disappointment was Martin Amis's *The Information* (having thrilled at his work); the surprising (and lasting) delight, Thomas Pynchon's *Mason & Dixon*. The Scottish writers I remember from before going to university were – school aside – Kenneth White, Brian McCabe, Emma Tennant, Candia McWilliam, Iain (M.) Banks and, of course, Alasdair Gray. All were in the displays of the long-deceased Talisman Books. (In terms of cultural ignorance, I did not realise it was named after a Scott novel). It seems in retrospect ironic that my first acquaintance with the work of George Mackay Brown was the unseen practical criticism paper at my Oxford interview (the poem was "Keeper of the Midnight Gate").

Returning to Scotland felt, in a way, like being late for a party to which I hadn't been invited anyway. This is admittedly impressionistic, but my memory is of a palpable buzz about Scottish literature. Through friends, librarians and the newspapers (at the time *Scotland on Sunday* had over 7,000 words of book reviews; it now has 1,200), I started catching up. The writers whose work interested and intrigued me were people like A. L. Kennedy, James Meek, Ali Smith, James Robertson, Andrew O'Hagan, Janice Galloway, Alan Warner – as well as less well-known writers such as Frank Kuppner, Alice Thompson, Andrew Crumey, Gilbert Adair, Bill Duncan, John Herdman, and the American-born Edinburgh residents Todd McEwen and Lucy Ellmann. Through the anthology *Dream State* I discovered many of the poets whom I still read. Likewise, the authors mentioned above are those whose new work I actively seek. They are all older than me.

No cultural phenomenon has a single cause, but there were a number of beneficial confluences at play. The history of this period would be very different without a figure like Peter Kravitz, firstly at *The Edinburgh Review* and then at Polygon, at the time an imprint of Edinburgh University Press. Much of the work first produced there would migrate towards Secker & Warburg and Jonathan Cape. At the same time Canongate established itself as a key part of the infrastructure. There was also a healthy literary magazine scene, with established titles like *Chapman* (in seemingly perpetual hiatus since 2002),

Cencrastus (which closed after the devolution referendum) and *Edinburgh Review*, which limps on intermittently. At the time I had subscriptions to at least half a dozen magazines, all on sale at Thin's in Edinburgh. I still have my copy of *Northwords #4*, which I acquired much later than its publication, and which had the first extract from *Morvern Callar*. Although a number of small publishers or imprints were set up, almost always dependent on Scottish Arts Council, then Creative Scotland finance (notoriously 11/9, but also Two Ravens, Sandstone, Freight, Cargo, Penguin Scotland), none proved sustainable.

This might be an unfashionable opinion, but I felt the uncertainty, the provisional nature, the ambiguity of devolution was more amenable to literary culture. Liam McIlvanney, a writer and critic whom I admire, has written about Scottish writing effectively and perhaps ineffectually declaring its independence, and there is much to commend in his argument. For a while, the "question of Scotland" was the prime subject of Scottish literature. For a while, for example, Janice Galloway could write about Clara Schumann. As Coriolanus realised, "there is a world elsewhere". The period immediately prior and after devolution was a series of questions and hypotheticals. When it came to the referendum on independence, everything collapsed into binaries. Complexity, nuance, ambiguity, being-in-two-minds, irony, uncertainty and disquiet – the very virtues of literature – were now questionable. This is not intended as a proof but an observation: after the September 11th 2001 attacks, there were eventually works of literary significance such as DeLillo's *Falling Man* (2007) or Ken Kalfus' *A Disorder Peculiar to the Country* (2006). A decade after the referendum, what do we have to show for it in terms of culture? Some bad agitprop, some trite slogans passed off as poetry, the occasional folk song that could be read as referring to the matter but worked just as well on its own. There was one growth area: the production of literary strategies and reviews. I still have my copies of "Review of Publishing" (2004), "Literature, Nation" (2009), "Literature Working Group Report" (2010) and "Literature and Publishing Sector Review" (2015). They are almost a genre of their own, these documents that produced nothing, like Rauschenberg's exhibition of an erased de Kooning sketch. Not entirely fair, as it did produce more bureaucracy. When the "Literature Alliance Scotland" formed, it represented the major bodies in receipt of Creative Scotland funding: Scottish Book Trust, Edinburgh International Book Festival, Publishing Scotland, the Scottish Poetry Library and suchlike. It has now – it may have voted itself out of existence before this piece appears and the whole carnival will have donned new costumes – twenty-four organisations and eight "network associates".

As the years went on, my initial enthusiasm seemed an echo of the "melancholy, low, withdrawing roar". I am adamantine that literature in general is no worse, and there have been many, many books it has been a dazzle and privilege to read. When I survey what is marketed as literary writing by the epigoni, I feel like Hamlet's father: "what a falling off was there!" There is an almost inverse proportion rule at work, in that the more vested voices declared a Renaissance, a Golden Age, an industry "punching above its weight", a tiresome cacophony insisting how strong Scottish literature was. Maybe Estonian or Senegalese or Laotian literature have similar cheerleaders of which I am unaware. The combination of a national debate about the political future and a slightly hyperactive literary rhetoric led to a false syllogism, that if you disliked a Scottish book, you disliked the idea of Scotland itself. Accusations of cultural cringe or tallest poppy syndrome were commonplace. I came across an almost funny example on Wikipedia, on the page for the writer Laura Marney, which claimed that she, along with Alan Bissett, Nick Brookes, Rodge Glass, Alison Miller, Zoe Strachan and Louise Welsh formed "The Glasgow G7 group of writers", an entity whose existence was footnoted to an article by Heather MacLeod, and a broken link. It is its only extant online presence. But it chimes with fantasies about MacDiarmid and the Poet's Pub, or Philip Hobsbaum's writing group at Glasgow University; hallucinations of a clique or movement that might be comparable to the Algonquin Hotel or Gertrude Stein's salon. New voices were "brave" and "urgent" and almost always transient. I have a large file of the once-lauded.

The immediate present seems to me to be profoundly dispiriting. Over the past few years I have had to undergo several operations for a condition I apparently have had since before birth, a volvulus of the intestines. The assistant surgeon made it frightfully clear to me as I signed the consent forms that my death was a very real possibility. In recuperation, reading, I realised that something might have been – indeed, one day something would definitely be – the last thing I read. It somewhat sharpened my temper. I do not wish my time to be wasted. I do not intend to name names here, but my overwhelming feeling is that a great deal of contemporary Scottish literature is simply not serious, however seriously it takes itself. Time and again I am reminded of the words of the great Australian Modernist, Ern Malley, in his poem "The Darkening Ecliptic": "I had read in books that art is not easy. / But no-one warned that the mind repeats / In its ignorance the vision of others." Much of the writing was derivative, and clearly signalled its influences, like pleading for a comparison. Reworkings of prior stories did not destabilise dichotomies but merely inverted hierarchies of value in a manner no more subtle or entertaining than the Two Ronnies' 1980s anti-feminist serial *The Worm That Turned*. A need to be modern often manifested itself merely as a desire to shock (in crime fiction, such out-doing still goes on in an unseemly fashion). But the shocks were still not as metaphysically shocking as, say, Brian Evenson or A. M. Homes, and frequently seemed more like Compo in *Last of the Summer Wine* threatening to show Norah Batty something gruesome in a matchbox. It seems natural that the counterpart of the supposedly raw and unflinching would be a curdled sentimentalism, which was evident in most, regardless of the extent to which they might be considered realist in tone or not. Closely connected to this tenor is the preponderance of narratives of triumphant victimhood. These are not stories of resilience or even overcoming, but victimhood as a kind of triumph, a form of pure affront. The moral, such as it is, is not – to use the 1967 words of therapist Thomas Harris – "I'm OK, You're OK" but "I'm OK and don't you dare say otherwise". It is a literature of self-validation and self-affirmation. Just as I do not believe in exceptionalism for the excellences of Scottish literature, nor do I subscribe its flaws to being uniquely or meaningfully Caledonian. I might almost take heart from the fact that narcissism, solipsism, moral grandstanding and the narrowly doctrinaire masquerading as liberal freedom seem fairly widespread. Kafka insisted "a book must be an axe for the frozen sea within us". It is not a sentiment I detect in many of the recent novels I have read.

You can vomit in a delphinium-scented kailyard, but it's still a kailyard. There are writers whose work I think admirable, and I have chosen a few based on their being memorable in an age of disposability and ones that I re-read. They were not exhausted immediately. There are others, but these seemed the most striking even on a first reading. I would have included Ewan Morrison, whose work has become stronger and stronger, and despite having been sceptical about his earlier work. His hybrid work *Tales From The Mall* convinced there was an adult in the room, and the loose trilogy of *Close Your Eyes*, *Nina X* and *How To Survive Everything* I consider very fine indeed. I have read an advance copy of *For Emily* and think it even better. All of them deal with characters negotiating being in someone else's narrative (a far cry from the "aren't stories magical" pabulum). But Ewan is firstly older than me and secondly a friend, and in my defence and I can say that I read him before I knew him, and now dread him writing a new book which I might not like.

When I was considering this piece, it seemed important to rely on my own memory rather intangible digital records; and likewise to note that as much as

I admire these works intellectually, the cerebral response is accompanied by a somatic one. These are books to which I had involuntary responses: a catch in the throat, a mist in the eye, horripilation, laughter. As Sontag realised, we might aspire to an erotics as well as a hermeneutics of interpretation.

Victoria Mackenzie's *For Thy Great Pain Have Mercy On My Little Pain* (2023), about the mystics Julian of Norwich and Margery Kempe is a study in different forms of radicalism: retreat against confrontation, silence against outspokenness, almost a classicism against a Dionysian form. Its excellence, however, lies in the ability to hold polarised positions in suspension, without the reader feeling the author's thumb on one or other side of the scale. Ever Dundas is the author of both *Gobin* (2017) and *HellSans* (2022) and both have a similarly stereoscopic vision. *Gobin* tempts the reader to read magic realist aspects as psychic prophylactics, fabular bandaging to the unbearable – or admit to there being more things in heaven and earth. *HellSans,* about a ubiquitous and possible demonic font, presents its narrative in two parts to be read in either order that will precondition how one reads the closure. Although Ali Smith has done something similar with *How To Be Both*, Dundas I think pips it with the idea of reading as a form of potential impairment. Jenni Fagan's debut, *The Panopticon* (2012) also uses the idea of the fantastical as necessary overwriting in its depiction of the vicissitudes of the care home system. There is a genuine honesty in creating, in the protagonist Anais Hendricks (a self-chosen perfume and a gin, and yes, Nin and Jimi are there too), an unvarnished female lead. *Luckenbooth* (2021) is her most ambitious, and although it doesn't quite equal *Cloud Atlas* or *Life: A User's Manual,* though sharing tropes with both, it retains her askance-ness and refusal to sanitise the avant-garde. (Its satire on Scottish literature is a rare quality). Ali Millar's *Ava Anna Ada* (2024) might allude to Nabokov, but its spiritual lodestone is more akin to Gombrowicz and Cocteau. The climate change temperature is both real and an effective pathetic fallacy for sultry game-playing and stifled grief. Again, in the blistering relationship between Anna and Ava there is a dangerous tango about controlling narrative, a topic very much in evidence in Millar's 2022 memoir, *The Last Days* about growing up in the Jehovah's Witnesses. J. O. Morgan is better known as a poet, but his debut, mainstream fiction, *Appliance* (2022) was a remarkable series of vignettes about a matter-transportation device. It is a limpid, painstaking book with a strange out-of-time air, as if reality were running on a reduced number of scan lines (by contrast, Ned Beauman's *The Teleportation Accident*, although serious, was more madcap and Technicolor). The ontological problems are properly moral problems, and a judgement on them is left in hiatus. Simon Stephenson also started in memoir, with *Let Not The Waves Of The Sea* (2011), then a delightful, tear-jerking comedy, *Set My Heart To Five* (2020) about an artificial intelligence who glitches from being a dentist to wanting to be a writer. Its deployment and subversion of screenplay formats and tropes is done charmingly, and bears comparison with Charles Yu's similar *Interior Chinatown*. *Sometimes People Die* (2022) was technically "genre" but its eerily sonorous prose and moral complexity – as well as humour: deaths in hospitals are hardly rarities – sets it apart from most of the form. (He also has a young adult novel, *The Snowman Code*, forthcoming). Ryan O'Connor's *The Voids* (2022) is ostensibly set in Glasgow, but it is really a bricolage of abandonment, desolation and detritus. The transplantation of the gothic into modern urban settings is notoriously difficult, but here it does cohere, particularly in the psychic dislocation of a character unable to escape place. The more surrealist parts owe something to William Burroughs in its necrotic consumerist imagery, but the idea that "the faintest human touch … everyday communion" is the portal into the abyss is wholly the author's own. Finally, Martin MacInnes: if anyone were to be the Scottish winner of the Booker after Kelman, I really wish it had been him, MacInnes has written three novel – *Infinite Ground* (2016), *Gathering Evidence* (2020) and *In Ascension* (2023). Each has been stronger, and his most recent is a staggeringly beautiful knot around the beginning of life, the bottom of the ocean, the edge of the solar system, faith and science as belief systems, what we value and why. It wryly incorporates Psalm 130 – "a song of ascension" – that begins "out of the depths", that admits none might stand against the evidence of their sins; and yet there is mercy. It is tour de force. That it is about tentative optimism makes me cautiously less pessimistic about literature from my native heath. In contrast to many of the other, often more prominent authors, these writers surprise me. They do not seem content.

One final appoggiatura. Scotland is not overburdened with comic literature, but it is a mere twenty-three years since the publication of Peter Burnett's *The Machine Doctor*. If you are lucky enough to find his fugitive pamphlets, *The Lanyard Strangler* and *Confessions of a Bobby Toucher* (about the famous Edinburgh dog, of course) consider yourself blessed.

Stuart Kelly is the literary editor of Scotland on Sunday *and a freelance critic and writer. He was raised in the Scottish Borders and studied English at Balliol College Oxford, gaining a first class degree and a Master of Studies. His works include*

The Book Of Lost Books: An Incomplete Guide To All The Books You'll Never Read *(2005)*, Scott-Land: The Man Who Invented A Nation *(2010), which was longlisted for the BBC Samuel Johnson Prize for Non-Fiction, and* The Minister and the Murderer *(2018). Kelly writes for* The Scotsman, Scotland On Sunday, The Guardian *and* The Times. *In 2016/17 Kelly was president of The Edinburgh Sir Walter Scott Club.*

A DISTANT PROSPECT

James Campbell

Alternative cities.

First, some random observations on being a Scotsman who lives in England.

The quickest way to make an enemy of me is to say, "You don't sound Scottish." Looking at things from the opposite direction, to ask, "Do I hear Glasgow in that voice?" or claim "I recognize that accent!" will carry you far.

My nationality has apparently burdened me with a birthmark: I am "a dour Scot". Not that anyone is likely to get personal over it. It's not about me. I am sometimes grumpy, occasionally sulky; once every four or five years I lose my temper. There are doubtless other failings. But dour I am not. I am, however, a Scot, and dourness is my destiny. Irishmen are no longer thicker than the rest of humanity, black people are seldom characterized by a sense of rhythm, Italians need never again be bottom-pinchers. But to be a Scot is to languish eternally in the realm of Dour.

I cannot count the times I have heard thrift (or the like) named as "the national characteristic". Usually, it is stated for my amusement. Suitably amused, I am prompted to reply that I have never met a people as mean as the English. This is no more true or fair than the original proposition. Frankly, it is silly. But it gets the required response.

I have never asked for "A weeee drraaam", though I am often offered one.

I have no objection to being addressed as "Jock", but "A weeee drraaam, Jock?" might change that.

When I set off for a trip home, I am not headed for "the frozen North".

I know what to think when I read in a memoir by a well-known English poet that "Hugh MacDiarmid and Robert Garioch were introduced to read their poems in Gaelic".

I am not an expert on everything Scottish: from the decision whether to write "the Stuarts" or "the Stewarts" to the habitat of the Crossbill or unruly weavers in early nineteenth-century Jedburgh. When I worked at the *Times Literary Supplement*, every book with Scotland, Scottish or Scotch in the title or subtitle, on any subject whatever, was placed on my desk. *Columba: Story of an Island?* "That'll be one for Jim." *Compositions for Viola in the Court of King James IV?* "Jim's desk is the one at the back."

On the other side of this old penny, I am apt to experience for any Scot encountered in London feelings without equivalent elsewhere in my emotions. I'm not being sentimental: the feeling might be dislike – but it's a different dislike. (This is perhaps the place to state that some of the kindest and most civilized people I have ever met are English.) At other times, it is akin to fellow feeling, even to family feeling.

In that sense, I am pleased to say that a good few family members dwell with me in London now. There is no danger of my being disowned by them, for they are all dead. At least two were born in the eighteenth century. But they maintain an ineradicable presence in my life, giving an awareness of continuity, as family does in general. The books they wrote and the music they played constitute a healing force I call on when mood demands it. Their headstones are big, sometimes three storeys high: they are houses where each of them lived at one time or another.

It will become clearer as we go on, but for the moment here are some names (alphabetically): Joanna Baillie, Catherine Carswell, Thom Gunn, Bert Jansch, John Martyn, Robert Louis Stevenson. Their closeness consoles me, in the way that emotional-support animals do. They have never really left the houses in which I found them, years or even decades ago, yet they are not frozen or ghostly. Something like the opposite: their being is stabilized. They are where I need them to be.

It is an eclectic assembly, likely to shrink or grow with time, but we are held together by the common thread of adoption by this city. Don't try to tell me that the twenty-three-year-old RLS no longer lives in that rented room in Hampstead I'm going to take you to. It will only force me into a contradiction. When I find him writing to a correspondent, "I passed a dog near Jack Straw's Castle looking out of a gate so sympathetically that it put me into good humour", I recognize not only the false-fronted pub on the edge of Hampstead Heath but the dog, too. That dog's sympathy has put me into good humour since I first encountered him in Stevenson's *Collected Letters*. He is a London dog, and from time to time a little bit of London me fondles his 1870s ears.

Something similar goes for Bert Jansch in Westville Road, in Shepherd's Bush. I heard his distinctive attack on the guitar the other day when I stood at the open door of the terrace house at No 17 and peered in at the carpeted staircase leading to up his dismal first-floor flat. I know where I was, aged fifteen, when I first watched my sister's art school friend play "Angie" on a fabulous gleaming instrument (in our Glasgow living room) and I know where he was when I last saw him in the flesh: walking along Westville Road at ten o' clock on a January night. With his London dog, as it happens.

A friend asked recently, having read something I wrote about travelling round Scotland in the 1980s, "Are you still a Scot? Or a Londoner?" No one in my position would hesitate over that question. A Scot, to the souls of my boots, if you'll allow the pun. But a Londoner, too, by mutual adoption.

To illustrate the point, and test the boots, I invited my friend to accompany me on a tour of Hampstead, to visit a few of these companions. We met at Belsize Park Tube station on Haverstock Hill and began walking north. A few incidental, unmarked monuments ought to be noted before we pass on. T. S. Eliot and Vivienne Haigh-Wood (a couple of Scottish names there, but let them go) were married at Hampstead Town Hall in July 1915. William Empson lived in a rambling villa with his family where Haverstock Hill blends imperceptibly into Rosslyn Hill. Further up, the novelist John Fowles kept a pied-à-terre when he became as miserably rich as Midas. The least known of these incidentals, I suspect, is the flat 200 yards further to the north where Leonard Cohen lived at the turn of 1959-60, on the corner with Gayton Road. He wrote part of his first novel, *The Favourite Game*, here. After gazing up at the window above the children's clothes shop Le Petit Bateau, you can cross the road and pop into Waterstone's to buy a copy.

Instead of doing that, my companion and I continue uphill, steeper now as we approach the highest point in Central London (440 feet above sea level) and come to Holly Bush, one of the gems within the jewelled cluster that is Hampstead itself. Directly before us, at a fork in the road, is Bolton House, where the Scottish playwright and poet Joanna Baillie (1762–1851) lived with her sister and stern Presbyterian minister father. *Plays on the Passions* had some success in the early 1800s. For Sir Walter Scott, on journeys to London, Hampstead was always "one of the most pleasant objects I have in view". It was not so pleasant on an occasion in 1811. He told Baillie how he had feared he was about to be mugged on the Heath after leaving Bolton House, when "the evening had nearly closed". Luckily, he had "a very formidable knife which when opened becomes a sort of *Skene-dhu* or dagger". The year before, Scott had manoeuvred her play *The Family Legend* on to the stage at the Theatre Royal on Princes Street in Edinburgh.

A Royal Society of Arts red plaque fixed to the front of Bolton House commemorates Baillie's residence "for nearly fifty years", after the family moved from Hamilton. Her name is not much mentioned now. In 1930, a biographer of Scott could refer to "the general oblivion that has descended on her name", and the situation hasn't improved.

While struggling to decipher the plaque's lettering above the high garden hedge, we glance to the right, taking in the short, right-angled street that is Holly Mount, site of the quaint Holly Bush pub. My friend had not heard of the Glasgow-born novelist and biographer of Burns, Catherine Carswell, and was interested to learn that the narrow Holly Bush House in the crook of the angle was once the home of Catherine and her husband Donald. Both worked for a time at the *Glasgow Herald*. Among Donald Carswell's books is *Sir Walter: A Four-part Study in Biography*. One of its parts is devoted to Joanna Baillie, and it is here that the reference to oblivion is found.

Immediately to our left as we turn from Bolton House is the steep, S-shaped ramp that bears the street name Mount Vernon. You can see it in the opening shots of William Wyler's film of John Fowles's first novel, *The Collector*, which he wrote not in the flat on Rosslyn Hill, where we last saw him, but in nearby Church Row. At the top, we approach Abernethy House, where Robert Louis Stevenson stayed on two occasions in the early 1870s. Hampstead was a separate borough in the foggy nineteenth century, and recommended as a haven for people with delicate lungs. Stevenson was one. In the summer of 1874 he and his friend Sidney Colvin "occupied jointly for a while a set of lodgings" in this handsome house. In 1902, the Hampstead Annual published Colvin's recollections of their stay. "Much else in the near neighbourhood has undergone transformation since those days", he wrote. "But this house remains the same." Some of the transformations of Colvin's time have themselves been transformed – a euphemism for demolished – but I am pleased to say with him, "this house remains the same". It hosts an oval-shaped, black Hampstead plaque, "Robert Louis Stevenson, Author, Lived Here", which suggests a more settled residence was the case. The word earns its place, however, by an anecdote that immortalizes Stevenson's stay.

One morning, Colvin noticed his friend leaning from the side window, looking on to Holly Place (a narrow downhill street out of view to the left in the picture), watching a group of girls with a skipping rope. Stevenson summoned Colvin to the window with a "radiant countenance … Was there ever such a heavenly sport? Had I ever seen anything so beautiful? Kids and a skipping-rope – most of all that blessed youngest kid who didn't know how to skip – nothing in the whole wide world had ever made him half so happy in his life before."

Here is Stevenson himself, from the essay he wrote about the scene: one of the girls, aged "from seven to nine perhaps", cradled in her arms "a fair-haired baby". Even so, "while the others held the rope for her, [she] turned and gyrated, and went in and out and over it lightly, with a quiet regularity that seemed as if it might go on for ever". What charmed him most was the arrival of an infant girl of about three, "looking for all the world like any dirty, broken-nosed doll in a nursery lumber-room". The others slowed the rope, so that she might do what they had been doing, but she lacked the necessary coordination and retreated, "putting up her shoulders and laughing with the embarrassed laughter of children by the water's edge, eager to bathe and yet fearful".

Much as he admired the grace of the older girls, it was the "clumsiness" of the little one that inspired "Notes on the Movements of Young Children" (included in later editions of *Virginibus Puerisque*). It would be inconsequential were it not so full of life – the life that took place where we are now. In the woodcut by Francis Colmer you can make out two or three children roughly sketched on the slope leading to the oddly named street, Frognal.

We pass the girls without disturbing them and descend to a darker prospect. In the early 1940s, at the corner of Mount Vernon and Frognal, lived the teenage Thom Gunn, his younger brother Ander, their mother Charlotte and father Herbert. Life for the family came to a sudden stop at 9.45 am on December 29, 1944, when Thom and Ander discovered their mother in the parlour. She had killed herself by inhaling from a gas poker. Efforts to bar the parlour door so that her sons would not be first to find the body were in vain. Gunn was fifteen. Fifty-five years later, he remained defensive of her. "My brother and I found her body," he told me in 1999, when I interviewed him in San Francisco for a series of BBC radio programmes, "which was not her fault because she'd barred the doors." Not long before then, he wrote "The Gas Poker", one of the few things he committed to print about his mother:

> They who had been her treasures
> Knew to turn off the gas,
> Take the appropriate measures,
> Telephone the police.

Thom Gunn, Scottish poet? Thom was not Thom at all, but William Guinneach Gunn, the middle name being the Gaelic form of the surname; so you could say he was W. Gunn Gunn. Both Charlotte Thomson and Herbert

Gunn were fully Scottish, from the North East. In an act pregnant with meaning, the son adopted his mother's maiden name in his later teens and cut it to the now distinctive form. In a letter of 1993, Ted Hughes wrote to him about a trip to Caithness: "I shall go into a tiny round graveyard on a cliff over the River Thurso in the NE of Scotland, where about thirty Gunns, under variously elaborate, marvellously lichen-patched gravestones... defend your ancestral bit of body-garden."

Gunn didn't feel Scottish, but he didn't feel English either. His adopted countries were, on the one hand, homosexuality – a territory with well-policed borders in the 1950s – and, on the other, a disguised grief. An "elaborate, marvellously lichen-patched" grief.

The brown Hampstead plaque on the side wall does not memorialize Charlotte's famous son. It is for E. V. Knox, editor of *Punch*, who "lived here from 1945 until his death in 1971". (Knox was the father of the novelist Penelope Fitzgerald.) The arrival date suggests that the house was sold immediately after the dreadful event. Thom and Ander never lived here again. Their father had left by the time Charlotte took her own life.

It is one of the oldest houses in Frognal, a street of architectural and historical treasures. On the wall above the plaque it might be possible to discern a niche where there was once a pub sign. Nos 110–108 Frognal used to house The Three Pigeons. Much later, No 108 was the home of the rock star Sting, which I suspect would have pleased Thom.

When pondering the parallel world to which these doors lead, I sometimes wonder what I expect from it. Nothing more than the suggestion of an alternative city, in which R. L. S. is forever patting a dog, Sir Walter promises a visit, Bert Jansch is strolling down Westville Road and Thom Gunn is soothing his wound with his great barking laugh.

There is no need to become ethereal about it. I like the city I live in. I miss the one I come from (painfully altered by the demolition ball) and the one I lived in after that, Edinburgh. I have visual projections of these former home towns to call on ... and I do here, too. My London would be emptier without them.

In a letter to an expected guest, Joanna Baillie wrote: "Our dinner hour shall be half past five, and if you are disposed to walk on the Heath, come to us as early as you please." It is exactly half past five now. Too early for dinner but not for "a ramble on the Heath", as Baillie put it elsewhere. After that, we make our way back down Rosslyn Hill, once again passing Hampstead Town Hall. If I don't have my wee dram by 6:30 p.m., I get a bit dour. Did I mention, by the way, that that old Glasgow troubadour John Martyn married Beverly Kutner in the Town Hall in April 1969?

James Campbell was born in Glasgow in 1951 and attended University of Edinburgh. His books include Talking at the Gates: A Life of James Baldwin *(1991, 2021);* Paris Interzone *(1994);* Just Go Down to the Road: A Memoir of Trouble and Travel *(2022). He worked for many years at the* Times Literary Supplement *and wrote the celebrated column "J.C". A collection of these appeared as* NB by J.C: A Walk through the Times Literary Supplement *in 2023.*

RECOVERY

James Robertson

Not a foreign country after all.

1.

"Recovery" is a good word. It stands for, among other things, coming through illness, trauma or calamity to a better place. It implies, more than just surviving, the regaining of strength, capability, hope, purpose.

"Recovery" can also mean getting back something that was lost, stolen or forgotten. Retrieval, restoration, rescue: it's not obvious to me that recovery has any negative connotations.

I've been re-reading some of Wendell Berry's essays. From his farm in Henry County, Kentucky, Berry has been sending out the same message for many decades. In "The Native Life", published in 1968 when I was ten, he writes:

> We have lived by the assumption that what was good for us would be good for the world. And this was based on the even flimsier assumption that we could know with any certainty what was good even for us. We have fulfilled the danger of this by making our personal pride and greed the standard of our behaviour toward the world — to the incalculable disadvantage of the world and every living thing in it ... We have been wrong. We must change our lives, so that it will be possible to live by the contrary assumption that what is good for the world will be good for us.

And this is from "Damage", published in 1974 when Berry turned forty and I was sixteen. He quotes William Blake's line from *Proverbs of Hell*, "You never know what is enough unless you know what is more than enough," and then he says:

> I used to think of Blake's sentence as a justification of youthful excess. By now I know that it describes the peculiar condemnation of our species. When the road of excess has reached the palace of wisdom it is a healed wound, a long scar.

A scar is a sign of recovery, of damage contained, accommodated or excised. The landscape is covered with scars; some the evidence of geological shifts, erosion, ice, flood, volcanic eruption; others made by humans. The exposure of archaeological remains is another kind of recovery, revealing to us how our ancestors lived and died, and it is usually undertaken with care, sensitivity and respect. But those words seldom apply to the methods used to exploit the planet's resources for industrial, commercial or agricultural purposes; and often it is nature, unaided by our species, that puts in the work that enables the land to recover from those abuses.

Wendell Berry's message, over fifty years, has become a stark warning. Stop behaving as we have done for the last two centuries, or it will soon be over for us.

2.

During those same fifty years I have been finding out about my country's history, languages, literature, music, art, architecture, ways of living – in short, Scottish culture – and I am nowhere near finished. Given the scale of the climate change crisis, discussion of Scotland's present and future political and cultural condition might seem almost inconsequential. But this is not a matter of either/or. The two issues are connected: as the personal is political, so the local is global, the national international. It is not small-minded to care deeply about what lies closest to home. The mindset of the metropolis can often be more parochial than that of the parish.

Wendell Berry's radical conservatism, his determination to return to farming practices that are less destructive of the land and especially of the precious topsoil without which agriculture is doomed to fail, reminded me of something Walter Scott had written in his *Journal*, and I went in search of it. Scott's *Journal* is a magnificent, lonely masterpiece, kept for the last six years of his life. Into it he poured his thoughts and feelings following his financial downfall and the death of his wife, whilst spending most of his days writing vast numbers of other words in order to pay off his debts. This he achieved, but at the cost of working himself into an early grave at sixty-one, suffering five strokes along the way.

Always a Tory in his political and social views, he became more reactionary in his final years; but even as he lashed out against reformers and (mostly imaginary) revolutionaries he remained sympathetic to the urban poor, who not long before had been the rural poor, and he was conscious of something going profoundly wrong with people's relationship with the land. This is the Berry-like passage I was seeking, in the entry for 20th February, 1828:

> The state of society now leads so much to great accumulations of humanity that we cannot wonder if it ferment and reek like a compost dunghill. Nature intended that population should be diffused over the soil in proportion to its extent. We have accumulated in huge cities and smothering manufactures the numbers which should be spread over the face of a country and what wonder that they should be corrupted? We have turned healthful and pleasant brooks into morasses and pestiferous lakes; what wonder the soil should be unhealthy?

But I was also drawn to something on the page before it, which I had previously missed:

> I have some distrust of the fanaticism even of philanthropy. A good part of [it] arises in general of mere vanity and love of distinction gilded over to others and to themselves [the philanthropists] with some show of benevolent sentiment.

That's a pretty accurate description of the, as it turns out, not so modern phenomenon of virtue-signalling. When I come across something like this my faith in the past is renewed. It is not a foreign country after all. We need to keep visiting it, engaging with it and especially with figures, like Scott, with whom we might think we have little in common, or who make an easy target for facile modern judgements. If we don't explore the past then how can we understand the journey that has brought us to where we are? This too – tracing the route – is a form of recovery.

Scotland's passage from a mainly pastoral and agrarian society to a commercial and industrial one was brutal, rapid and relentless. In that transition an entire peasant class, the cottars – perhaps as much as half of the rural population – was lost forever. They and tens of thousands of even poorer people were forced off the land across the Lowlands, Highlands and islands. They ended up in towns, cities and planned villages, they worked in mills, mines, quarries and ironworks, or they emigrated to other parts of the world, or became soldiers, sailors, engineers, administrators and merchants in the service of the British Empire or the companies that thrived under its bellicose protection. Many prospered, many did not.

Yet despite these enormous changes, and despite now playing an integral part in the great imperial project, Scotland remained Scotland. Some of its leading cultural figures tried to be North Britons, but the English were not in the least bit interested in becoming South Britons and after a while the Scots realised that they sorely wished to retain their own characteristics even if these had to be hammered into new shapes fit for new times.

Through his poems and novels Walter Scott, among others, provided a recipe for how to be Scottish in the 19th century: a sense of history, an appreciation of beautiful landscape that had once been thought ugly and menacing, hard-headed commercial Calvinism and romanticised Highlandism were all in the mix. It worked brilliantly for the next hundred years, began to be challenged in the wake of the First World War, and crumbled rapidly in the later 20th century with the end of Empire and the demolition of its successor regime, the British Welfare State, by the very political and economic forces which had previously believed, or claimed to believe, in both.

Hugh MacDiarmid, writing in 1943, attacked Scott's fiction as "the great source of the paralysing ideology of defeatism in Scotland, the spread of which is responsible at once for the acceptance of the Union and the low standard of nineteenth-century Scots literature." As so often with MacDiarmid, who wrote his own prescription for how to be Scottish, there is truth in this claim as well as hyperbole. I happen to have a high regard for both writers, but again this is not an either/or dichotomy. One of MacDiarmid's slogans in the 1920s was "Not Traditions – Precedents". Implicit in those three words is an acknowledgement that precedents have to come from somewhere, and if not from traditions then from where? It's what you do with the inheritance that matters. Do you stick it in a kist in the attic and let it moulder, do you copy it in ever-paler imitations until all you are left with is pastiche, or do you learn from it, appropriating and remaking what will be useful for your own times? Even if you want to smash it to pieces, knowing how it is constructed is handy in order to make the demolition most effective.

Edwin Morgan's poem "King Billy", from *The Second Life*, his breakthrough collection of 1968, ends with these instructive lines:

> Go from the grave. The shrill flutes
> are silent, the march dispersed.
> Deplore what is to be deplored,
> and then find out the rest.

We must be familiar but not comfortable with the past. We have to challenge it as it must challenge us, whether we're dealing with the legacies of sectarianism, slavery or imperialism: these are not unconnected from us, nor from one another. But we should recognise, without complacency, the valuable as well as the deplorable. It's what we cherish most that really boosts recovery.

3.

Does each generation have to learn everything all over again?

Maybe so. In every era, people discard, destroy or neglect what they inherit, only later to realise that much of what they thought broken, useless or unworthy of care was not. This is not a specifically Scottish problem, if it is a problem, although being "a mouse in bed with an elephant" (a phrase coined by Pierre Trudeau in 1969 to describe Canada's relationship with the United States, but applicable to Scotland's neighbourly association with England) can complicate things. For example, one of the drivers in the growth of the Scottish independence movement in the last half-century has not so much been nostalgia for some golden Caledonian age but a regret for the passing of the British state as it existed for thirty years after the Second World War. It may well have been the case that we were "better together" in that period: certainly, people of my vintage, the baby boomers, know that we were, and remain, the lucky generation. But that model is broken. The Tories under Margaret Thatcher deliberately deconstructed it, Labour under Tony Blair stuck some of it back together, but neither of those parties is proposing to do that again: no progressive taxation system, no reform of the electoral system, no serious investment in public services and, in case anybody is in doubt about which bedfellow calls the shots, no reversal of Brexit. The elephant is unwell. The mouse, on the other hand, might recover if it gets out before it is flattened.

I'm thinking about all this partly because of my age. I recently became a pensioner. How on earth did that happen? It seems only yesterday that I was a ten-year-old charging into the North Sea breakers. Now the tide is on the way out. I'm not depressed about this. Ageing is what happens, it's a natural process and, as a wise woman once said, "Never regret growing old. It's an experience denied to many." Nevertheless, the health you once took for granted – if you were lucky enough to be healthy – begins to let you down. You lose strength and agility, both physically and mentally, and although you can work against the decline it takes increasing effort.

But, oddly enough, another aspect of ageing is recovery: recovery of some deep memories while others, shallower and less valuable perhaps, are deleted almost instantly; recovery of a story, how you got from childhood to here. I started life in Sevenoaks, Kent, one outcome of three Scottish grandparents going south after the First World War. When I was six, my father got a job that brought us to Stirlingshire. Had that not happened, I would have been the same boy genetically and physically, but I would have grown up to be a very different person, shaped by a different set of experiences and, crucially, by a different culture. Almost from the moment of that flit, I have held the view that Scotland would be a better place for its people if it were once again an independent country; if the United Kingdom as presently constituted no longer existed. I also believe this would be better for the other parts of the United Kingdom. Everything that has happened since the 2014 referendum (including the General Election that took place in July this year, after this essay was written) reinforces that belief. Recovery of Scotland's independence will not make a great difference to me in the years I have left, once the celebrations are over. But for the generations that follow, faced with the overriding issue of climate change and how to build a sustainable human relationship with the planet, I think it will.

Having knowledge of our past, being able to appreciate that inheritance and what bits of it to deplore, what bits to value, will be essential for that new project, just as it was for the projects of Walter Scott and Hugh MacDiarmid. They will be vital aids in the recovery.

I'd like to conclude with a poem, written by Kathleen Jamie, the estimable Scottish editor of this journal, that distils into twelve lines what has taken me more than two thousand rambling words. Poetry may not make anything happen, but it tells you how it might.

The Tradition

For years I wandered hill and moor
Half looking for the road
Winding into fairyland
Where that blacksmith kept a forge

Who'd heat red hot the dragging links
That bound me to the past,
Then, with one almighty hammer-blow
Unfetter me at last.

Older now, I know nor fee
Nor anvil breaks those chains
And the wild ways we think we walk
Just bring us here again.

James Robertson was born in Sevenoaks, Kent, England in 1958. He took an MA Hons in History and a PhD in History, both at University of Edinburgh. His publications include The Fanatic *(4th Estate, 2000);* Joseph Knight *(4th Estate, 2003);* The Testament of Gideon Mack *(Hamish Hamilton, 2006);* And the Land Lay Still *(Hamish Hamilton, 2010);* Republics of the Mind: New and Selected Stories *(B&W Publishing, 2012);* The Professor of Truth *(Hamish Hamilton, 2013);* 365: Stories *(Hamish Hamilton, 2014);* To Be Continued *(Hamish Hamilton, 2016); and* News of the Dead *(Hamish Hamilton, 2021). He is currently working on a new novel. He is also a general editor and contributing author to* Itchy Coo, *a Scots language imprint for young readers which he co-founded in 2002. He currently lives in Angus, Scotland.*

LOSING OUR RELIGION

Fraser MacDonald

A diasporic sense of self.

There's an ordinary question that should be easy to answer: "where are you from?" I don't like it because too much hangs on the preposition. "Where are you?" is straightforward. "Where are you from?" demands a history and a geography, a biography and a backstory, and these are things that have to be composed rather than stated. My usual answer is that I'm from Aberdeen, more specifically, I grew up in the village of Cults in Lower Deeside. Yet I don't like this answer because it doesn't say anything about the community of my childhood which was less a place than a church. The Free Church of Scotland in Aberdeen was – formal education aside – the entirety of my world. My father was its Session Clerk for nearly fifty years. Ministers came and went but my parents were its anchor until they died close together at the end of 2019. My father's funeral was the last time I was in the church. It showed me how much this world had changed. A funeral marks the passing of a life but there is no equivalent ritual for the passing of a way of life.

Their church was in the city but, only to a limited degree, of the city. It claimed descendance from the eighteenth-century Aberdeen Gaelic Chapel and while worship was now in English, the congregation in the 1970s and 1980s was still significantly comprised of Highlanders and islanders. Congregational life embodied the religious norms and rhythms of the *Gaidhealtachd*: Psalm singing without instrumental accompaniment, extemporary public prayer, Sabbath observance, Communion seasons, midweek prayer meetings, preaching that was expository and heartfelt and often intelligent. It felt like a world on its own, an island almost, amid a sea change of liberalism and secularism that had left Free Church congregations scattered like an archipelago across Scotland's major cities. Even in my youth, us "Wee Frees" were a recognisable national species – rare, yes, but still holding our own in the heartland of the Highlands and Islands. Presbyterianism more broadly – not just our own variant that was conservative, evangelical and Calvinist – felt like an element of the national psyche. It represented an older moral order, a little anachronistic at times, with a homespun religious certainty that worked as a kind of foil or cultural signature, something to disavow or push against, even as its presence was a living reminder of the Reformation. In my early childhood, growing up in the Free Church of Scotland made it difficult for me to see it, or to understand it. I was simply inside it – it was the rest of Scotland that seemed strange. I did sometimes envy my school mates' freedom: they had Sundays for trips or projects, they had clubs and hobbies; they didn't have to learn the 107 responses within the Shorter Catechism, or sit yearly examinations on scripture and psalmody. I don't recall resentment that my life was different, but by the age of ten I encountered the reality that we were rather different. The very idea of cultural difference was a formative realisation.

One summer's day in 1982, we arrived home to our house to find a box on our doorstep. It had been left by the minister, Rev. Hector Cameron, who was clearing out the manse after moving to another "charge" in the Black Isle. The contents of the box, entrusted to my father's safekeeping, were wrapped in white sailcloth and contained the Kirk Session minute books going back to the Aberdeen Gaelic Chapel. The opening line in the first book read: "In the year 1785, A great number of Highlanders, from different places, who resided in Aberdeen, lamented that they have not the Word of God preached nor divine ordnances Administered in their own language." My father was the first generation in his Highland family not to speak Gaelic: his unwillingness to learn concealed the mundane ways in which his "outlook" – a favourite word of his – was caught up with the language. Something about the struggle to worship in one's native tongue moved him. He laid out the minute books on the kitchen table, his finger underlining the fine English copperplate on stained parchment that recorded the rudiments of congregational life: new members, baptisms, accounts, session debates. He told me that these minutes and ledgers contained the story of displaced Gaels making their way to quarry granite in an east coast city while holding fast to the religion of their ancestors (doubtless this was also an appeal to me to walk in their ways). In October 1985, he organised a commemorative weekend of services to mark "two hundred years of the Highland Congregation in Aberdeen". One of these services left a deep impression on me: the worship returned to Gaelic and it was a revelation to see how readily our church assumed its original guise. The old psalmody evoked other places and times, from the waters of Babylon to the cleared straths of Sutherland, as if this other mode lay just under the surface, dormant and unused, yet could be summoned in memory of our ancestors. The Scottish novelist Eona Macnicol (her people hail from the same crofting township as those of my father), once described Gaelic psalm singing as:

a curtain of sound, a fabric woven of many gracenotes ... held suspended on pauses, shaken when ... other voices joined in. [...] What human grief, what dire need, what poignant hope and waiting for consolation were interwoven into that singing. [...] Long after it had faded from the air, it hung shivering in the spirit.

Gaelic psalm-singing is now usually a performance that ends up on stage or on television, or marks the closing of a cultural event. In the twenty-first century, it has become a self-conscious aesthetic form that is easily valorised because it is functionally moribund. It wasn't like this in my childhood. Our English language psalmody that used the 1650 Scots Metrical Psalter often carried intonations and elongations from its Gaelic equivalent. The absence of an organ meant that our praise rose and fell on tides of feeling: solemn and restrained for psalms of contrition, full and expansive for psalms of exaltation. Scottish Presbyterians are not known for euphoria but there were times when it seemed that the roof slates rattled with the fulness thereof. The vista from our pews may have been pitch pine under 60 watt incandescent lights and Belling bar heaters, yet we sang as if eternity stretched before us like unfolding nebulae:

> Ye gates, lift up your heads on high;
>   ye doors that last for aye,
> Be lifted up, that so the King
>   of glory enter may.

Psalm singing and extempory public prayer could be regarded as Scottish folk cultures were it not that the guardians of folk, like the collectors at the School of Scottish Studies, had decided early on that they were not much interested in religion. Hamish Henderson referred to it as "the dithering, degenerate black Calvinism of our own day". That didn't matter. We occupied a different temporal plane. Sometimes after an intense sermon, our evening worship might conclude with the closing verses of psalm 72: "His name for ever shall endure; last like the sun it shall ..." which is exactly how I thought of our own cultural world. This isn't an exaggeration: it would have been easier to imagine solar extinction than to contemplate life without rising in unison to sing these shepherds' songs. That's not how it turned out.

Scottish Presbyterianism is not dead, neither in its liberal or conservative evangelical incarnations, yet the changes I have seen in my own life are so far-reaching as to bring about a sense of unmooring and loss. Everything feels different even when it's hard to get the measure of what, exactly, has changed. The obvious expression of these changes is the list of church buildings currently for sale – sanctuaries, burial grounds, manses, and halls. They are not obscure buildings but monumental sites that are the backdrop to our social history and yet here they are on the open market. In Aberdeen: the local landmark of St Mark's Church of Scotland, an iconic granite-pillared neoclassical edifice in the city centre, now costs less than a suburban home. In Inverness: the Old High Church was only built in 1770 but the site is arguably the birthplace of Christianity in northern Scotland and first appears in a charter from *Alasdair mac Uilleim*, Alexander II, King of Alba in 1240. It's available for offers over £150,000. So many churches have already been re-purposed. My own local church, Portobello Old Parish Church, where Scottish geologist Hugh Miller once worshipped, is now Bellfield community centre – a successful example of adaptive re-use. But the sheer flood of available buildings makes it hard for communities to absorb. The story of our cities is always of buildings at odds with the time of their making. We have learned to make peace with the defensive architecture of castles and walls, garrisons and arsenals. That's an easy heritage, perhaps. Churches are different. They are not just monuments to power or to labour but to feeling itself; they are the grounding of our need for transcendence; they mark our collective emotional past of enthusiasm and terror, shame and pride. It's an adjustment to realise that so many of the intensities – the peculiar religious affects – of Presbyterianism no longer exist. The last vestiges of the Scottish sabbath have lifted in my lifetime. Most people will not miss the departed restraint and quietude but I still register the liberties that I now take on a Sunday. A spot of DIY with a noisy circular saw? No problem. A cycle of laundry to be hung on the line? Of course. Yet the loss is my own because there's no pause; there's just life's maelstrom – the kids and the garden and that work thing I need to do – and it's hard to hear the mantel clock measuring time and eternity.

 I miss the feelings of an evening service. The pews of my childhood were a site of the sublime, of heights and depths, of horror and uncertain comfort. As a young adult, when I read Edmund Burke's 1757 treatise on the sublime, it all seemed so familiar: "whatever is fitted in any sort to excite the ideas of pain, and danger, that is to say, whatever is in any sort terrible, or is conversant about terrible objects, or operates in a manner analogous to terror, is a source of the sublime; that is, it is productive of the strongest emotion which the mind is capable of feeling." And I wondered if the Anglican Burke had ever adhered to a hard Scots pew – did he ever experience the perfect bond of sweat, cotton and varnish that came from learning that there is not even a false hope in hell? A theology founded on "wide is the gate, and broad is the way, that leadeth to destruction" gave the future a particular tint. It perhaps accounts for a strain of Caledonian gloom but it also made life seem short and vital.

There are aspects of these changes that make me rejoice. We can cheer, for instance, the deposed humiliations of the cutty stool – furniture for fornicators – a practice so grim that you might think it impossibly ancient, like witchtrials or heresy, but my grandfather was raised by an aunt who had her time on the stool and the experience echoed down the generations. There is nothing to miss about this moral economy of shame, even if it is premature to think that it has fully lifted. Homophobia may be less blatant, and more openly resisted, but it's still there in the background. In my childhood, even the Free Church of Scotland's most liberal minister, the theologian Donald Macleod, complained in the church magazine that Aberdeen Central Library was making a newsletter, *Gay News*, available to readers over the age of sixteen. That was in 1978. Much has changed in the culture of conservative evangelicalism but the anxiety about sex – and its dwindling indexicality to "traditional" marriage – is its distinguishing theological constant.

In other respects, however, the church no longer fits the caricature of a forbidding killjoy quite as well as it once did. The Free Church I grew up in variously condemned Elvis, bingo, bagpipes, Sunday newspapers, women wearing trousers, the Pope, Sunday ferries, Satanic backmasking on vinyl records, pubs, dancing, hymns, organs, women elders, free contraception and Frankie Goes to Hollywood. But even here much has changed. Many of these things are fine now – okay, not women elders – but the church has become less formal, more urban, more diverse and professional, and more weighted to the central belt rather than to the Highlands. The change is reflected in its corporate logo: while the Church of Scotland has kept the 1691 emblem of Scottish Presbyterians – the burning bush with the motto *Nec Tamen Consumbatur* [it shall not be consumed] – the Free Church has a stylised version that looks more like my early attempts at latte art. It is keen to be modern. While many churches are sitting on a demographic time-fuse, evangelical congregations tend to be more resilient, their numbers buoyed by shared symbols and identity-markers – opposition to trans rights, say, or to abortion – that clearly draw the boundaries of inside and outside.

The most significant changes are not strictly theological. There have been few revisions to the underlying ideas about Biblical inerrancy, or about the univocality and divine inspiration of Scripture – rather, the changes are to the cultural and aesthetic forms of worship. There's been a move away from singing Psalms; praise bands have become common; Gaelic worship scarcely exists, even in places like North Uist which was once its stronghold. The King James Version of the Bible and the old Scots Psalmody have been shelved for more accessible translations like the New International Version. The hush and formality of a traditional service has given way to an air of convivial chat. Hard pews have been replaced with individual upholstered chairs. These are more comfortable, though my father didn't see it that way. He had a reputation for being thrawn, but some of his resistance to these changes came from an assertion of cultural distinctiveness – he felt that the religious customs and habits of his people encoded their diasporic sense of self. This was who they were.

He was particularly disappointed at the waning of the common cup for communion. Our congregation had four silver beakers, two of which were fashioned in 1819 as a gift to the Aberdeen Gaelic Chapel from its outgoing minister, Rev Duncan Grant. The cups are large and silver and generally needed two hands to lift, especially when full. Their unadorned style mimicked that of ordinary drinking vessels rather than the ornate goblets of the pre-Reformation church. With due solemnity, the cups were filled with port and passed along the pew. Each member would lift the cup, drink, and pass it along for it be received by an elder in the aisle who would redirect it along the next pew. The cups never touched my lips – for I was never a communicant member – but how often I saw them up close on our kitchen table as my father would polish them. He did this for half a century until the folk in the pews grew squeamish at the passing of a shared cup. Individual cups felt safer, and more in keeping with concerns about pathogenicity, but they deprived my father of a sense of unity and connection to the past. "What a privilege it is" he wrote to me, "to handle a cup that links us to pilgrims who trod the same road in [a] former day just as its contents likewise links us to the Saviour of the world." That cup has passed. It belongs to a different time, and to a different landscape of feeling. I miss it. I don't miss it.

Fraser MacDonald was born in Aberdeen in 1972. He was educated at University of Glasgow (BSc in Geography) and Oxford (MSc, DPhil). He writes for the London Review of Books. *He is the author of* Escape From Earth: a Secret History of the Space Rocket *(Profile, 2019). He is currently writing a book on the problem of wildness. He lives in Edinburgh and teaches at the University of Edinburgh.*

NOTES ON A SCOTTISH FEMINIST AESTHETIC

Catriona McAra

A poetics of sowing ideas.

One of the challenges of writing a new art history of Scottish women artists is that the very possibility of the topic comes with an implicit inclusivity agenda: to write such a book, means the author is somehow obliged to comment on every single creative woman working today on Scottish soil. I have already lost count of the number of commentators who seem to hold this expectation (and double standards). But completionism is not my project, nor should a collective effort to intellectualise women be the responsibility of one individual. While such an undertaking would, of course, be impossible from a practical standpoint, it would have a limited lifespan and purpose. Griselda Pollock insists that any feminist art history rewrite the rulebook and that it is the task of my generation to nuance the broader-stroke contributions of her own (*Vision and Difference*, 1988 [2003]).

Femininity is a controversial terrain (and to be a Scottish lassie still carries its own peculiar set of structural biases and mythical expectations). While increasingly porous, let's not forget that gender remains a cultural, social and historical fact shaping the way women (artists) have been differently seen, educated and interpreted for centuries. Laura Mulvey has long maintained that feminine-coded myths (of Pandora, selkies and such) might be recoded into a feminist politics (*Topographies of Curiosity*, 1996). Or, in artistic terms, that the recognisable traits of traditional feminine media (softness, petals, domestic still life and weaving) are now metamorphosing for twenty-first century purposes in the hands of some of Scotland's leading artists.

So, what might constitute a Scottish feminist aesthetic? Art that speaks to the mind as much as the eye while offering a women's experience and changing the viewer's mind may be a preliminary definition. As with any worthy project, meaningful criteria must be established: to rewrite an art history shaped by the art itself as well as by the gender of its maker. What it will have to be is a curatorial selection of the mid-career, professional artists (artists who make their living primarily from their art) who have gone through the Scottish education system and/or chosen to base themselves in Scotland and achieved international recognition in the 25-40 or so years during which they have been practicing. So, who are the "great" women artists living and working in Scotland? Or rather, which artworks are most representative of advanced art by women based in Scotland and working internationally today?

For the purpose of this brief critical experiment, a curated dialogue between two contemporary artworks that draw from national history comes to mind as bearing the hallmarks of a Scottish feminist aesthetic, one abstract, the other representational: *The Edinburgh Seven Tapestry* (2024), a soft sculptural triptych celebrating the first seven women-medics to matriculate in Scottish higher education (1869), and *Lindsay* (2019), an oil painting of a cut-rose, a visual quotation of a detail derived from Allan Ramsay's portrait of his second wife, *Margaret Lindsay of Evelick* (1758–1760). Let me begin with the art before I discuss the artists. Both *The Edinburgh Seven* and *Lindsay* include intricate details which appear to float on minimal backgrounds. *Lindsay* is based on a local rose specimen known as "Lady Hamilton": its petals are depicted with infinite variety and wrought skill to offer a visual discourse on the capture of light as a form of painterly problem-solving – Ramsay's portrait itself is luminous and appears to glow from within. *The Edinburgh Seven* is similarly loaded with visual data and site-specific meaning. Elaborate, speckled and organic forms are punctured with voids pulsating with life and genetic coding. I see them as embryonic thought-forms. *Lindsay* and *The Edinburgh Seven* offer homage and *memento mori*, an acknowledgement of the transience of opinion too. They are paradigm-shifting, markers of change.

What have *Lindsay* and *The Edinburgh Seven* to say to each other? Probably rather a lot about putting the world to rights, of rebalancing gender discrepancies, of detailing and reviving reputations. For historical agency and visibility for women are core to the principles behind both artworks which have both been acquired as part of nationally significant collections (the former commissioned for Edinburgh Futures Institute [EFI]; the latter purchased for the National Galleries of Scotland and already something of a Scottish icon). Central-belt-centric these choices may be, yet they stand for wider bodies of work that have been shown across the country and beyond. Their makers know and respect showing in Perth, Inverness, Argyll and Bute as much as in the major art capitals.

If I choose to highlight these two artworks for this definition, it is not because they are pretty, pink and sentimental but rather because they are cerebral, technically accomplished and historically informed. The makers of *The Edinburgh Seven* and *Lindsay* share more common ground than one might expect. They are exact contemporaries who have achieved international recognition: Christine Borland and Alison Watt (both born 1965). Borland is lauded for her medical inquiries often realised through object-making (e.g., ceramics, glass hanging or shadow play) with more recent forays into the language and history of plant textiles. Watt, meanwhile, is best known for her drapery paintings with more recent investigations into the genre of still life, traditionally a domestic possibility for women yet appearing at a lower level in the seventeenth and eighteenth-century "hierarchy of genre" which Watt seeks to revise (Gen Doy, *Drapery*, 2002). Crucially, both artists take their medium and genre through the lessons of twentieth- century modern art and revise it for contemporary purposes. What intrigues me is that both are unapologetically feminine in their daring choices of artistic subject matter and processes (flowers and yarns) *and* astutely political in attitude as public figures. They are unafraid of using their work as a space to explore what it means to be a woman maker (an arena that was distained even as recently as my own art education c. 2007). Claire Raymond suggests that "Feminist aesthetics indicates a political act in image" (*Can there be a feminist aesthetic?* 2017). Ergo, the veneer of a Scottish feminine aesthetic swiftly reveals its feminist clout.

Given their very distinctive approaches to artmaking, one is struck by the overlap of Watt and Borland's educational foundations. Both went through The Glasgow School of Art at a crucial moment in the mid 1980s: Watt in Painting and Borland in Environmental Art. While many commentators will position these two departments as oppositional (one programme concerned with medium, the other with positioning the idea), I would argue that there is a consistent and longitudinal quality to the practices of both that stems from their art educations at GSA. Writing in 1971, feminist art historian Linda Nochlin lamented the lack of access to the nude, a chief pedagogical mode of inquiry in the academies, as the primary barrier for the possibility of women artists obtaining a fully rounded education (*Why Have There Been No Great Women Artists?*). Historically, life drawing, that most basic of apparatus, was allowed only to male students. Conversely, by 1988, Watt was one of the only students at GSA who was still working with life models. Watt was steeped in rigorous and traditional training in studio practice with faculty including Barbara Rae (b.1943). Although Rae's colourful landscapes are starkly different from Watt's artistic concerns, Rae offered Watt a local, living exemplar of a professional woman painter, a fact which cannot be underestimated in the predominantly male department of the time. Meanwhile, Borland had the benefit of studying under the wing of feminist artist and pedagogue, Sam Ainsley (b.1950) whose guest-speakers included Susan Hiller (1940–2019) and Adele Patrick (b.1961). Ainsley's ability to teach and justify context and concept became paramount, more so than materials and techniques. Ainsley recalls phoning various institutions, such as medical departments, to enable this process: "Can my students come and look down your microscopes?" (*In Conversation*, 2024). A cross-pollination of such approaches is now becoming apparent across the Scottish art scene, and Watt and Borland are two figureheads for successful practices that have stemmed from both schools of thought.

Greenock-born Watt is now based in a studio in Edinburgh's new town after a stint as fellow at The National Gallery in London; Ayrshire-born Borland now resides in Kilcreggan and holds a chair at Northumbria University. I do not suggest that a Scottish woman artist need only be a working-class intellectual (but it is a start). Nor must they remain tied to practicing in the big cities – both artists have undertaken residencies in rural Aberdeenshire and beyond. Neither is "Scottishness" in the artworld an exclusively white endeavour – some of the nation's best artists (if selection to represent the nation at the Venice Biennale is anything to go by) whom I might well have chosen for this article, were born in Barbados (Alberta Whittle, b.1980) as well as Alexandria (Karla Black, b.1972). Like Watt and Borland, both Whittle and Black have work in national (and international) collections, and their practices arguably develop the aesthetic, conceptual, and technical inquiries of the generation under discussion. Whittle's raffia-fringed dreamscapes and cowrie shells, and Black's cosmetic sculptural matters (eye-shadow and bath-bombs) are further examples of what we might start to recognise as a national feminist aesthetic.

For both Watt and Borland, inquiry and curiosity are innate qualities of their resulting artworks, whether prompted by art history in Watt's case or the medical humanities for Borland. Both share an interest in the very fabric of artistic practice and in the poetics of sowing ideas. A process of unlearning and detaching from the status quo in order to reframe and question can be perceived in both. A revision of the still life genre for Watt might be aligned with Borland's rethinking of traditionally feminine crafts such as porcelain and tapestry (Sarah Lowndes, *Social Sculpture*, 2003 [2010]). It is perhaps no surprise that both artists, given their status, have undertaken commissioned projects at Dovecot Studios – one of the last safe havens for experimental practice in the country. Both raise clever, timely and nimble gender queries through their medium. Their artworks possess an apparently effortless lightness of touch but are often more than meets the eye: "Much of my work is about the transformation of an object into an idea", Watt claims (*Hiding in Full View*, 2011). Indeed, I would suggest that Watt's paintings are far more conceptual than many people realise. Commenting on Watt's *tableaus vivants* (living pictures) of the mid-1990s, Clare Henry was among the first to note this trajectory:

> Minimal white bowls, clothes, studio. Simple elliptical shapes. Ambiguous body parts in a minimal setting. Could Watt be the first figurative painter to make the leap to figurative conceptualism. I think she could. (*Clare Henry Papers*, 1995)

Contra-wise, Borland's art harnesses a keen interest in form and material as well as idea. Curator Katrina Brown observes that Borland is versed in "translating invisible information into some kind of legible form" (*Progressive Disorder*, 2001). Thus, Watt and Borland share an ability to pare back their aesthetics, to isolate what matters. As Borland has said of her own practice:

> The use of a minimalist aesthetic as a presentational mode is deliberate. It starts as something reductive because that's what science does to information and then I take on the riches in my conversations with researchers and practitioners in that dialogue. Then I distil (and yes) often end up reducing them again on the way to making a piece of work. (*In Conversation with Craig Richardson*, 2009)

Borland's *Edinburgh Seven* recently went on permanent display at EFI (a former hospital) after touring to the V&A in London where it hovered appropriately above a statue of St Margaret and the Dragon, St Margaret being a patroness for pregnancy. *Edinburgh Seven*'s unique triptych format includes magenta, turquoise, vermillion and carmine-black areas of woven textures, referencing dyes which would have been available during Victorian-era medical practice for staining (*Dovecot Studios*, 7 March 2024). The forms further mimic the cellular structures which might be perceived under a microscope. Here, a knowledge of visuality is overlaid with the history of women medics entering the academy. Borland used motion capture to sculpt the tapestry into shape, with the artist herself performing simple gestures associated with medical training such as bandaging to capture the flow of the fabric (Carol Richardson, *Weaving the Edinburgh Seven*, 2024). One might be inclined to associate similar biomorphic and uterine shapes with Lucy Lippard's soft-sculptural "eccentric abstraction" (1966) as found in the work of Eva Hesse (1936–70) and Louise Bourgeois (1911–2010), an aesthetic Lippard went on to discuss during the Women's Liberation Movement (*What is Female Imagery?* 1975). Borland readily acknowledges Lippard and other American avant-garde touchstones. While this may suggest that the feminist avant-garde experienced a delayed reception across advanced Scottish artmaking, arguably it needed the right educational grounding and the generation to realise it.

Watt's *Lindsay* first appeared in her major solo show *A Portrait Without Likeness* (2021) at the Scottish National Portrait Gallery. This marked a new departure for Watt, two decades since her solo show, *Shift* (2000), at the Scottish National Gallery of Modern Art. After many years spent studying French neo-classical drapery, Watt turned her attention to a Scottish Enlightenment precedent in the form of Ramsay. Watt acknowledges a keen interest in the "proto-feminism" of Ramsay's portraits of women (*In Conversation with John Leighton*, 2021), not only the idiosyncratic ways in which the sitters are shown, but the peculiar accoutrements with which they chose to self-present (a broken rose or cabbage leaf cradling hazelnuts). Watt suggests that such a still life *objet d'art* becomes a personal museum which has much to say about its owner. Thus, for Watt, groups of objects offer a metaphoric mode of portraiture (one without strict illustrative "likeness"). Writing on objects of nostalgia such as the miniature and the souvenir, Susan Stewart reminds us that the feminine is positioned socially against institutional authority (*On Longing*, 1984 [1993]). This perhaps explains why a feminine aesthetic has long been dismissed by the artworld, its refusal to fit neatly into formal categories. Again, once the feminine comes to consciousness as activated (and activist), it becomes useful as a feminist pursuit. This seems true of the success of Watt's *Lindsay*, a broken blossom, and its wider cycle realised through *A Kind of Longing* (2023). Watt's still lives function best in neo-classical architectural settings for a very good reason: they oppose authority by creating their own.

While Watt achieves her "portraits without likeness" by reviving the ancient representational language of *trompe l-oeil* (trick of the eye), Borland does so through digital perceptions. The Scottish feminist aesthetic is highly tactile and corporeal as well as drawing on the history of visuality. The tapestry uses cellular forms as a self-perpetuating pattern, referencing the kind of visual material the *Edinburgh Seven* medics might have studied under a microscope (a nod to Borland's own art education under Ainsley). Borland's body interacts with the material properties of the tapestry which reminds me of Watt's own physical experiments with the folds of calico and other drapery – a manipulation and scaling up of the physical source material contributes to a process of abstraction underpinned by an appreciation of satisfying proportions learned from antique drawing (*In Conversation with Keith Hartley*, 2000).

In writing these notes, I wanted to rethink how we cultivate a Scottish feminist aesthetic. Having now practiced for 40 years or more, Watt, Borland and their contemporaries have carefully propagated the achievements of the second feminist wave (Ainsley, Nochlin, Lippard, Pollock *et al*). I would suggest what we have with Watt's *Lindsay* and Borland's *Edinburgh Seven* are exemplary test cases of what such an aesthetic might be and what it might do. These artworks are microcosms for a Scottish feminist turn, representing new layers of demystification, acceptability and possibility.

Dr Catriona McAra is an art historian and curator based in Scotland and working internationally. She is a leading authority on feminist-surrealism having published books on Dorothea Tanning and Leonora Carrington. Her books are The Medium of Leonora Carrington *(MUP, 2022) and* A Surrealist Stratigraphy Of Dorothea Tanning *(Routledge, 2017). She is currently writing a third book on Scottish contemporary women artists, scheduled from Edinburgh University Press.*

STORIES-SO-FAR

Amanda Thomson

And the stories yet to come?

I'd always seen Loch A'an in part, in varying shades of blues and greys and always at a distance. It's a loch I'd long aspired to get to, but looking at the map and the tightly packed contours that surround it, I'd always felt too intimidated. Nestled within the Cairngorms, it lies 725 metres high, and you have to go up and over the Plateau to get down to it. It's a loch made famous by Nan Shepherd's *The Living Mountain*, a touchstone for so many of us for how she writes with so much care and attention about the area. The Plateau itself has always felt more within my capabilities and I've seen dotterel, snow buntings, ptarmigan, mountain hares, eagles and peregrines; the black-centred creams of dwarf cornel, the purply-pinks of moss campion, the greens and yellows of alpine lady's mantle, the bright pinks of mountain azaleas that miraculously hold butterflies and bees at 1000 metres high; all of these in an environment that makes you feel expansive and hopeful, and oh so small at the same time.

In her foreword to *The Living Mountain,* Shepherd observed that, from when she wrote the book in the 1940s to when it was eventually published in 1977, "many things have happened to the Cairngorms ... Cairn Gorm grows scruffy, the very heather tatty from the scrape of boots (too many boots, too much commotion, but then how much uplift for how many hearts)." It's the uplift to the heart that resonates with so many of us that go to such places but I wonder, in the years from 1977 until now, how many more boots, and bikes and e-bikes have ventured up, how much more worn have Cairngorm and areas like it become? What might the next 30 years bring?

When I finally made it down to the shores of Loch A'an it was in the company of about forty people, part of a project to restore a rare and endangered habitat. This area used to be one of the strongholds of a montane woodland habitat made up of specialist species of willow and birch, but in recent times it's been overgrazed and dangerously depleted, with any remaining plants cooried away on the steep slopes, burn-sides and cliff edges where deer, hares, even sheep, can't reach. The populations had become so dispersed that chances of cross-pollination were very small. These "willow walks" are culminations of long processes that involve collecting downy, whortle-leaved and eared willows from across their wild populations, propagating and growing seedlings in a tree nursery until they are large enough and strong enough to be replanted in areas around Loch A'an as well as other sites. These species of willow are short, stubby and perfectly adapted to grow in this high, extreme environment, and we carried thousands of them to plant and re-invigorate the area around the loch.

We made our way up from the fankle of the ski runs and the currently (or until recently, as we go to press?) defunct funicular that scars its way up Cairngorm itself. Up and beyond Cairn 1141, so-called because of its altitude, a 360-degree panorama takes you north over Abernethy Forest to Morayshire, south and south east to Perthshire and Deeside and west over the Monadhliath mountains. In the clear blue air, you can feel like you're on the top of the world and, aside from the paths, it feels almost untouched and unchanging. Yet the plateau is home to a variety of rare alpine plants that are threatened not just because of too many boots but because of how a changing climate – warmer temperatures and less snow cover – will change its very nature.

Nan Shepherd walked for leisure, solace too, perhaps, and for a "place of ease", and while this is what resonates with so many of us, it can't be the whole story of such places and how we see them. We have to listen to a multiplicity of voices, past and present, to make sense of who and where we are. The lowlands and uplands of Scotland were and are working landscapes, peopled places, even if historical events and seismic changes like the Highland Clearances and the Industrial Revolution, world wars and economic crashes as well as smaller, incremental changes affected ways of life forever.

So many places, from the Borders to the Highlands and Islands, hold evidence of transhumance – when livestock was moved from one place to another depending on the season. There are thousands of the remnants of the summer sheilings – buildings and shelters found in the high pastures where people would take their animals in the summer to keep them away from their other crops. Shepherd herself talks about coming across the remnants of shelters, crofts and hill farms and her novels write of rural life. Desmond Nethersole-Thompson and Adam Watson note that on Deeside there were sheilings up to about 2,000 feet and in Strath Avon there were sheilings on the hillsides right up to Loch A'an itself[1]. In archaeological surveys of sheiling sites, whisky stills and corn kilns have been found, speaking to the lives lived in these places that most of us see now just in passing. Shepherd's and hunter's huts are now mountain bothies and stone formations in the middle of nowhere were fanks that held livestock on journeys to or from markets. Many of the paths we walk now were drove or fish or even coffin roads. I wonder if, in, how we travel, how we *use* now, there's a sense of removedness that isn't doing well for us.

Some of us are lucky enough to live in places that might be considered "remote" or at the back of beyond by others, and many of us go walking in places without quite knowing fully who owns where we walk. Freedom to roam, for the most part, means we don't often have to seek permission to get out onto the hills or into the lochs, and so often we are only in the places that we love and that move us, fleetingly. Who we are and what we've been taught affects our perspectives in so many ways, and the histories of these places and how they have come to be as they are, are often lost.

While we can never go back to how it used to be, I'm struck by this quote from MacKinnon and Mackillop, who have written on the history of land and landownership in the Highlands in the past three hundred or so years:

> This increasingly one-dimensional use of the land stands in stark contrast to the mixed arable and pastoral economies of the *bailtean* which, in turn, sustained socially complex communities. These township populations nurtured knowledge production systems that enabled mixed land management strategies. This was underpinned by communal, rule-based approaches to foreshores, grazing, and fuel assets which were taken to be common pool resources. Local resources could then be exploited through a consciously integrated and diverse set of micro-economies.[2]

Fascinatingly, they also link some of the shifts in Highland society that occurred in the eighteenth and nineteenth centuries to the transatlantic slave trade and the benefits that some Scots, and Scotland gained from their involvement in it – whether as slave-owners, or through the associated cotton, tobacco or cotton trades. They consider this involvement, evidenced still in street names, monuments and buildings in many of our towns and cities, in relation to the Highland Clearances and what they call "external, globalised (or imperial) forms of capital", tracing some of the patterns of shifting land ownership in the Highlands to the compensation made to the owners of plantations for loss of "property" (i.e., those who had been enslaved), which then became invested in Highland estates. MacKinnon and Mackillop estimate that such compensation created a "slavery elite", many of whom evicted more (perhaps way more) than

5,000 people from their land during the Clearances. Exploring the complex patterns of landownership and inheritance, including traditional landholders marrying into slavery wealth, "it transpires that at least 1,834,708 acres of the west Highlands and Islands – more than half of the area's total landmass, and approaching ten percent of the total landmass of Scotland – has been owned by families that have benefitted significantly from slavery."[3]

They speculate whether some of the elements of exploitative, extractive mentalities that characterised the plantations of the Caribbean and other areas was brought to bear on the people, communities and the land that came to be owned in Scotland (though, of course, one cannot diminish the horrors of enslavement, the middle passage or plantation slavery, and must also ask, what of the behaviour of Scots to the indigenous people they encountered after their own forced removal from their lands and their emigrations to other parts of the world?). MacKinnon and Mackillop also contend that the influx of this wealth and some of the attitudes that came with it "[was] at the heart of the 'Victorian hunting cult' and of re-creating the highlands as a playground for the rich".[4] I think of this additional complexity in relation to all that James Hunter explores in his book, *The Other Side of Sorrow*, and his consideration of the ways in which the balance between people, land, nature and the environment was lost or negated during the eighteenth and nineteenth centuries, including attempts to extinguish Gaelic, an important language of connection. Hunter explores how the new narratives created by new landowners and the romantic notions of the highland landscape, replicated in the art and literature of the time, erased in large part the people, and the rich, complex and age-old heritage and way of life that still existed even as these new narratives came into being.

Andy Wightman's research suggests that landownership has become even more concentrated in the recent past. By his calculations, "half of all privately owned rural land in Scotland or 3.2m hectares (7.9m acres), is held by just 433 people and companies, with only 2.76% of rural Scotland held by community groups."[5] I'm wondering how might perceptions of the size and scale of ownership and the sometimes depersonalised nature and the perceived distance from local knowledge and heritage, rub up against histories of displacement and disenfranchisement, even when some of the larger landowners – including wildlife charities these days – see their ownership, even their interventions, as being benign and indeed positive (vital conservation work, protecting species under threat, habitat restoration including the vast peatlands so important for carbon storage). I wonder about this not even on the level of changing legislation and land reform, but on personal, visceral, perhaps psychic levels. The very speed, size, scale and complexity of the world often feels in conflict with the questions of agency, voice, stewardship, even, sometimes, generosity of spirit, and how we might or should see *ourselves* as custodians of the country, and, indeed the earth, for future generations. How do the demands (and some might argue sometimes wrongly placed senses of entitlement) of humans abut against the needs of the other species and habitats so important to the nation's health? And how do the needs of other species and the earth itself abut against the infrastructure that our everyday lives so often now demand (travel, holidays, the food we expect to be able to eat, the internet, streaming, Cloud storage)?

Recently I've been spending time at Ravenscraig in Motherwell, making a film-essay for "A Fragile Correspondence", the Scottish collateral exhibition at the Venice Architecture Biennale in 2023. More recently I've been back making a "summer" film for the iteration of the show in the V&A Dundee in late 2024. It's the site of what was Europe's largest steelworks, a mile square in size and closed down by Thatcher over 30 years ago. While there's new housing and a huge leisure centre on part of the site, most of it remains as it was left after demolition and clearance. Ravenscraig feels completely opposite to the walk up and over to Loch A'an, but I've come to think of it as another story that needs to co-exist with those of elsewhere. I'm reminded again of McKinnon and Mackillop's phrase "external, globalised (or imperial) forms of capital" and the far-reaching implications that it has for all of us; how removed decision-making can be from the people and communities that it affects.

When I first walked the site in winter it was the mosses that caught my attention – how bright and alive they felt in the dreich November light. While we could still see the remains of the steelwork's infrastructure – the ghost circumferences of the cooling and gas towers – swathes of the site were taken over by grasslands, birch and willow. Saplings and fuzzy lines of moss grew in the cracked seams of the concrete. I was amazed at how much nature had reclaimed. In the summer its footprint is vibrant with the whites of ox-eye daisies, yolk-yellow bird's-foot trefoils, kidney vetch and bitter stonecrop. Tangles of tufted vetches, yellow rattle, orchids, willowherbs, wintergreens and many other plants bloom. Rarities like yellow birds-nest nestle beneath birch leaf litter. Crows squabble, finches charm, starlings murmur and skylarks soar and fall to earth.

The architects/curators of the exhibition talked about the grain of the land being almost but not quite, north to south, and we walked the lines of the cooling and gas towers, access roads, strip mills and coke ovens. The idea of a grain is something that has stuck with me, understanding the way the land lies and why. They argued that whatever "development" of the site comes next, it's important to retain some kind of acknowledgement of what had been before.

Ravenscraig's closure may feel like a long time ago for some, yet at an event held in Motherwell in 2023 to introduce the project and at another for the exhibition of the work shown in Motherwell itself in 2024, it was clear how present it was for many of the folk of Motherwell still. How locals were affected by the plant when it was open – including its dangers and toxicity as well as the community it provided – and in the long shadow of its closure; how *ingrained* and intertwined identity was with the steelworks, how let down local people felt in the build up to its closure and in its aftermath, and also, how anger was harnessed and still felt. Even now, going forward, it's clear how questions of future "redevelopment" (and what that actually means) sit in tension with the needs and opinions of many, and where and how might questions of nature and conservation sit when what's first and foremost in people's minds might be housing, lack of services, support and everyday survival in the face of poor pay or un-employment and a cost of living crisis?

Nan Shepherd observed "thirty years in the life of a mountain is nothing", and though this might be the case in terms of its underlying geology, above and just below the ground, say in the peat layer, what changes might 30 years bring? A closure of a steelworks and its aftermath. In the past 25 years, swallow numbers are down by a quarter and the State of Nature Report for Scotland noted that of the 407 species monitored since 1994, abundance overall has fallen by 15%. While some species have increased in number or distribution, there are frightening declines for others. "Since 1994, swifts, curlews and lapwings have all declined in abundance by more than 60%, while kestrels have declined by more than 70%." Since 1970 there has been a 47% decrease in the distribution of flowering plants. It's disturbing to see that the report concludes:

Centuries of habitat loss, over-exploitation, the intensification of farming, development, invasive species and persecution (killing of wildlife) means Scotland is one of the most nature-depleted countries in the world, ranking 28th from bottom out of more than 240 countries/territories in terms of the biodiversity it has remaining.[6]

I'm often seduced by old Scots language words from nineteenth-century dictionaries and I marvel at how many seem to demonstrate a much closer affinity to and awareness of nature and the land than it feels like we have now: *May gobs*, "cold weather in the second week in May"; *lamp' o the water*, "phosphorescence on the sea"; *cock's-eye*, "a halo around the moon that indicates stormy weather". It feels like nowadays our immediate link to nature through language is more lost than found. Now we have other words coming into our vocabulary like *ecocide*, the destruction of the natural world, and *solastalgia* defined by Collins as "unease and melancholy caused by the destruction of the natural environment". Eco-anxiety.

The word precarious feels apt for when we think of the threats to our natural world, from the dangers of "too many boots" to the climate emergency, but precariousness is a word that taps into us at all levels, with ageing, cost of living increases, Covid, the rise of far-right extremism… I'm old enough to remember Section 28, which prohibited "the promotion of homosexuality", and the fight to repeal it. Even though Scotland is a safe place in relation to other parts of the world (for most of us at least), we have a devolved government that's recently reneged on its climate targets and a deputy first minister who said she would have voted against equal marriage laws. We're also in a country where the writer Hannah Lavery was compelled to write the play *Lament for Sheku Bayo*, about the death of this young black man who died in police custody in Kirkcaldy.

This essay feels speculative, partial, with more questions than answers. And I write about history, nature and the climate and everything else all too aware of social inequalities and the crises in our health and education sectors; our broken economies and political systems, regionally, nationally, globally; wars, occupations and genocides; and what needs done on a daily basis, just to get by.

While I am able to see some of what's wrong, and while I might be able to see what some of the solutions might be, I don't know how to get to where we need to be. I am not a strategic thinker or an effective debater. I get tangled up. I can see the small-scale movements and actions that can be effective and meaningful but don't see how to change, disentangle a world that feels excessively extractive and consumptive, where good ideas seem to get co-opted and corrupted by vested interests, a world that is racist and discriminatory, to a more sustainable, sensible, equitable trajectory.

The geographer Doreen Massey imagines spaces as containing "a simultaneity of stories-so-far" and I like that way of thinking about Scotland – the idea of simultaneity, what is happening, and has happened, from the micro to the macro every second of every day, across a' airts and pairts – urban, rural and in-between. The idea of *so-far* makes me think of Scotland's reach into the world, and the reach back of the world and all that happens in it to Scotland, as well as how it reminds us that we are not yet at the end, and there are multiple stories still to be written. I wonder what we want these stories to be; how we can highlight and activate the stories inscribed in the landscapes that are hidden, lost, or undervalued, and how we add them to those which have become mythologised and make the connections that need to be made. How might we fully acknowledge and deal with the long afterlives and consequences of the transatlantic slave trade and Empire, all that's come since and all that it has meant for how we see ourselves, others, and the world? Who, even, do we mean by "we"? How might we meld the histories that help explain who we have become to what needs done for the protection, care, support and recovery of Scotland's natural environment, people and communities too, as well as the rest of the world beyond.

What needs done to give us a sense of agency and stewardship; to listen and feel listened to; to help us navigate, sometimes, the differences of opinion that exist at local levels, never mind beyond. To deal with grey areas and nuance, competing values and competing demands? How might we truly incorporate these complicated stories and histories that are written into the very fabric, the very grain of the land, and how might we want to define not just the stories-so-far, but the stories-yet-to-come? And we have to actively want to listen, to learn, and learn from.

For me, the small act of tending, of carrying, of planting, is a start, a hope and a restorative act, communally held. Writing and art-making are also acts of attention and connection. Others find different plans of action. All are important. That a rare montane habitat might be re-established, whether or not I am alive to see it, and that peatlands I might never see are restored in ways that save and protect us (in a global sense, even), are some of the things that I hold onto, even if, at the same time, I struggle with questions of trust and power and powerlessness that are rooted in historical and global circumstances that sometimes seem impossible to fathom.

I want to think that we will find a way that we can come together in this ever-increasingly complicated world. I wonder the ways in which we might find the collectivity within our diverse circumstances, histories, geographies and experiences, how we might find a way to hold all that needs to be held, together, in order to create and connect the stories of Scotland that, in the future, we would like to be told.

NOTES

1. Desmond Nethersole-Thompson & Adam Watson, *The Cairngorms*, Collins, 1974
2. https://www.communitylandscotland.org.uk/wp-content/uploads/2022/08/Report-2020-Plantation-slavery.pdf
3. https://ehs.org.uk/plantation-slavery-and-landownership-in-the-west-highlands-and-islands-legacies-and-lessons/
4. Dr Iain MacKinnon & Dr Andrew Mackillop, *Plantation slavery and landownership in the west Highlands and Islands: legacies and lessons, A Discussion Paper*. Community Land Scotland, r 2020.
5. https://www.theguardian.com/uk-news/2024/mar/23/land-ownership-in-rural-scotland-more-concentrated-despite-reforms-study-finds#:~:text=Andy%20Wightman%2C%20the%20land%20reform,Scotland%20held%20by%20community%20groups
6. The State of Nature, Scotland, 2023, https://stateofnature.org.uk/countries/scotland/

Amanda Thomson is a visual artist and writer who lives and works in in Glasgow and Strathspey. Much of her work – in art and writing – is about the Highlands of Scotland, its landscape and nature, and how we are located (and locate ourselves) in the world. Her first book, A Scots Dictionary of Nature, *was published by Saraband Books in 2018.*

IN SEARCH OF SARMATIA:
ON THE TRAIL OF JOHANNES BOBROWSKI

David Wheatley

Stravaigs in time.

When I think of Scottish-German connections, I think of Walter Scott's 1816 novel, *The Antiquary*. Set in a thinly-veiled version of Arbroath, the book centres on an eccentric scholar, Oldbury, who when not expounding his theories on Roman remains in Scotland likes to remind us of his German heritage. His background has sensitized him, to a perhaps morbid degree, to intercultural connections. Like many a Scott character he spouts liberal amounts of Latin, and outlines to a young friend his schemes for a patriotic epic poem, *The Caledoniad*, on the battle of Mons Graupius — forgetting in the heat of the moment that the battle was won by the Romans.

I often think of Oldbury as I crisscross my own portion of the Scottish North-East, slightly higher up than Arbroath and, like Scott's Oldbury, am given to viewing the landscape through a German prism, specifically the work of Johannes Bobrowski (1917–65). To open his *Shadowlands: Selected Poems* (Anvil, 1984) at random is to find myself mysteriously shadowed on my stravaigs between the Don and Dee. Here is a stanza from his "Counterlight", first published in his 1961 collection *Sarmatische Zeit (Sarmatian Time)*, its lone wanderer scouting for revelations under a bird-torn sky:

> But
> who will bear me,
> the man with closed eyes
> and angry mouth, with hands
> that hold nothing, who follows
> the river, parched;
> who in the rain
> breathes the other time,
> which comes no more, the other,
> unspoken, like clouds,
> a bird with open wings,

> angry, against the sky,
> a counterlight, wild.

Bobrowski was born in East Prussia in 1917. He was active in the religious resistance to the Third Reich but served as a lance corporal on the eastern front during the war, until his capture in 1941. After 1945 he spent another four years in a Russian Gulag before returning to what is now East Germany. He died in 1965: "an early death", as his translator Michael Mead comments, "but not untypical in his broken generation."

The Sarmatia of *Sarmatian Time* is a notional kingdom in Eastern Europe, somewhere in the marchlands of Prussia, Poland, the Baltic States and Russia. As a historical conceit, it serves the obvious purpose for Bobrowski of allowing him to swap one place for a historical version of itself, the better to write about an impossible present. While the plains and market towns of central Aberdeenshire have not been racked by warfare anytime recently, I nevertheless find the affinities compelling. North-East Scotland is a place where many languages have rubbed up against one another, historically: English, Scots (Doric), Gaelic, Latin and Old Norse. Cultures come and go: once among the most Catholic regions in Scotland, it is now among the least. Conflict certainly is present, historically. Far from the central belt, the North-East was a stage for the Marquis of Montrose's campaigns in the 1640s, while the unsettled North-East of the following century bristled at the Hanoverian settlement, incubating instead the 1715 Rising. But just as Bobrowski's work swings between rumours of war and an almost mystical state of non-event, the North-East has its torpor too, the placid pastureland and dreary steeples against whose backdrop the twentieth-century presence of Lewis Grassic Gibbon (born in Auchterless, near Turriff) and Hugh MacDiarmid (who wrote *A Drunk Man Looks at the Thistle* in Montrose) seem so joyously anomalous.

A typical Bobrowski poem has numerous distinguishing fingerprints. There is a vagueness as to time. Lines are short, line-breaks jagged, like drystone walls suddenly rearing up at the edge of a field ("Counterlight's "hands /that hold nothing"). Syntax is elliptic: verbless sentences abound; pronominal coordinates are uncertain. Something awful may be going on but, as often as not, this is not reason enough for the poem to quicken its pulse. The population density is low: lone farmers appear scything in fields and fishermen raft down Lithuanian rivers, but the crowd, the tribe, the nation are elsewhere. In "Always to be Named" Bobrowski strolls through his Eden naming things into being:

> The tree, the bird in flight,
> the reddish rock where the river
> flows, green, and the fish
> in white smoke, when darkness
> falls over the wood.

But it is a strangely reluctant Eden, since:

> Were there a God
> and in the flesh,
> and could he call me, I would
> walk around, I would
> wait a little.

Some shadow of guilt taints any hint of pastoral innocence. That shadow has a name: wolf. "Across the steppe / wolves travel" ("Call"); "the hungry wolves" ("The Roads of the Armies"); "With green eyes / your wolf-time is lost" ("Vilna"); "The old wolf, / fat from the burnt-out site, / startled by a phantom" ("Lake Ilmen 1941"); "Near the drift, / lay the wolf, disembowelled" ("Death of the Wolf"). What could these predatory figures in the landscape be, Elizabeth Myhr has wondered, if not SS death squads rampaging through Eastern Europe. "It is impossible to verify whether or not Bobrowski participated in war crimes and atrocities", Myhr writes, but "he certainly witnessed them". In "Kaunas 1941" we read of the "grey processions of old men and boys" who "walk over / the hill" and "die there". The poem ends with the speaker walking along a riverbank and thinking of the coming night, before concluding "My dark is already come". It is a bleak and chilling anti-revelation.

The poet to whom Bobrowski is most often compared, Paul Celan, knew a lot about these wolves. What must he have made of Bobrowski's work, in the moment of their postwar emergence – so similar to his own, yet so crucially different. Bobrowski was far from the only writer in Celan's orbit whose actions during the war must have been sources of private anguish: in 1953 he translated his fellow Romanian E. M. Cioran's *Précis de décomposition* into German, despite (or quite possibly in innocence of) Cioran's wartime support for the Romanian Iron Guard. While Cioran engaged in histrionic disavowal of his youthful folly, Bobrowski is far less forthcoming. Yet directness does break through, on occasion, as in the chilling "Report". A young Polish Jew named Bajla Gelblung escapes from the Ghetto to fight with the Partisans. She is captured and photographed being interrogated by some German soldiers. Bobrowski writes:

> the officers are young
> chaps, faultlessly uniformed,
> with faultless faces,
> their bearing
> is unexceptionable.

It is a poem as profound as it is superficially offhand. Great evils are implied, but left to hang in the air unspoken. The poet is inspired by a photograph, despite writing of a conflict where such scenes would have formed part of the reality all around him. The role of the narrator comes under heavy pressure without, again, these moral challenges being spelt out. One thinks of the close of Geoffrey Hill's "September Song" ("This is plenty. This is more than enough"), another poem which stages an elaborate counterpoint of statement and silence.

My Scottish Sarmatia has nothing to compare to this, but I am drawn to those wolves as reminders of the fallenness of Bobrowski's eerily placid landscapes. The poets of my region inhabit their own historical shadowlands, zones whose obscurity makes them all the more alluring to my roving eye, and not without concealed guilts of their own. Sadly there is no Hugh MacDiarmid walking trail around Montrose, St Cyrus and Johnshaven, though at least MacDiarmid is in print. Older local poets are more likely to be found in castles than in bookshops. Violet Jacob (1863–1946) was born Violet Kennedy-Erskine at the House of Dun, now a National Trust for Scotland property, where lines from her poems adorn the tearoom walls. Further to the north is Baldorney Castle, where Gaelic poet Sìleas na Ceapaich (1660–1729) lived after her marriage to the Duke of Gordon's estate factor; her lament for Glengarry (*"Alasdair a Gleanna Garadh"*) is one of the great elegies of the eighteenth century. Nor is she the only Gaelic poet hiding in the landscape. Iain Lom (c. 1624–c. 1710), most bellicose of highland bards, wrote odes on the capture and death of the Marquis of Huntly in the 1640s. His vision of Scotland is ontologically Catholic, Stuart and Gaelic (*"A làmh a sgaoileas gach tonn duinn, / Cuir duinn Cromall a stalcadh"*/"Thou whose hand dispensed the wave, / Grant that we trample on Cromwell"). Aberdeenshire's falling away from these lofty standards today would no doubt inspire one of the thundering denunciations in which that poet's work is so well stocked.

Born slightly earlier, Arthur Johnston (c. 1579–1641) is, alongside George Buchanan, one of the two great Latin poets of the Scottish Renaissance. His work is drolly Horatian, for the most part, but strikes a darker note in a long poem on an act of arson in which the Gordons of Frendraught Castle were burned alive in 1630; injustice cries to Jupiter himself for vengeance. Johnston lived in Keith Hall near Inverurie and was the leading figure in a school anthologised in the *Delitiae Poetarum Scotorum*, whose work no one, or next to no one reads today. One of these bards was David Leitch (b. 1608), who has the distinction of being the only notable resident listed on the Wikipedia page for my village of Kemnay. He was a noted epigrammatist and participant in the fevered church politics of the day before deserting his ministry sometime in the mid-1650s and disappearing. And then there is Alexander Craig of Rosecraig (1567–1624), author of "Amorose Songs" and an elegy for an Irish poet called Yeats.

The thought of a Yeats writing in the seventeenth-century Scottish northeast rather than modern Dublin is deeply "Sarmatian", as I choose to understand that term. Sarmatia is space of displacement, transformation, reimagining. What was once urgent fades, not to the sepia of nostalgia but something closer to a mysterious mezzotint, such as Scott's Oldbury might inspect in his library. The violence and guilts of history too fade, but remain imaginatively available beneath the deceptive calm of my present-day landscapes. In seeing these landscapes through Bobrowski's eyes, I am least of all engaged in cultivating a persona; I feel less an identification than a counter-identification across an impossibility, a constant decanting of the past into the present and back again.

It is evening and I am standing at the edge of the village on a bridge over the river Don, with visible in the distance the sun sinking Morven and the Buck of Cabrach off to the west. I think of a stanza from Bobrowski's poem on his own river Don:

> The river was white. The higher
> bank dark. The horses
> climbed up the slope. Once
> the banks opposite
> fell away, we saw,
> behind the fields, far,
> under the early moon, walls
> against the sky.

The foreclosure of his panorama into those "walls /against the sky" is unexpected, inscribing confinement as well as openness into his closing epiphany. I wonder how high his hills must have been. The highest of the hills round my village is just under 1,800 feet, with the peaks in the distance continuing to rise until the eye reaches Lochnagar, gateway to the high Cairngorm summits beyond that again. A modest valley of the imagination then, self-sufficient but with drove roads around its edges for the poetic traffic I have tried to describe.

Boy racers on their motorbikes are noisily tearing up and down the long straight road to Leschangie on the other side of the village, and in the woods off behind me a tree has grown up straight through the middle of a bicycle someone once draped over a sapling. A swan flies over my head and language too is imperceptibly on the move, a language, as Bobrowski wrote:

> worn out
> by the weary mouth
> on the endless way
> to the neighbour's house

David Wheatley was born in Dublin in 1970. He was educated at Trinity College, Dublin and has published numerous books, most recently Child Ballad *(Carcanet, 2023) and* The President of Planet Earth *(Carcanet/Wake Forest University Press, 2017). He has also published four previous collections with The Gallery Press:* Thirst *(1997),* Misery Hill *(2000),* Mocker *(2006) and* A Nest on the Waves *(2010). He lives in rural Aberdeenshire and is a Professor at the University of Aberdeen.*

NEW SCOTTISH POETS

FOREWORD

Niall Campbell

This year, 2024, marks ten years since the last anthology of "New Scottish Poetry", Colin Waters' ambitious *Be the First to Like This*, and a fine thirty years since Donny O'Rourke's wonderful *Dream State* anthology that introduced so many of the poets who would go on to decorate the UK cultural scene. That it now feels a right time to renew such a project extends not only to falling so neatly into the sequence (1994, 2014, 2024) but also from what might be felt as a change in the weather in contemporary Scottish poetry itself.

It is perhaps tough but warranted to say that the past decade, perhaps two, were lean years for new voices in Scottish poetry who have made a significant mark on the artform. While such an observation maybe unfairly compares these recent poets to the high-water marks of those poets emerging in the 80s and 90s, and without wishing to burden with over eagerness or hyperbole, I do feel we are again seeing the emergence of a generation with significant promise – and, equally interesting, a generation of such varied modes, approaches and registers.

Currently, due to Covid backlogs, cuts in funding, and the complications of sustaining a readership in this digital age, it is more difficult than ever to acquire a publisher. It is a scenario that asks questions of how the London-based presses might be failing poets and writers outside of the south of England – and one that also asks why Scotland's own cultural sector is not being bolstered to fill this void. Still, it is heartening to see that a number of these poets have already stood out enough to make that first step of publishing a first collection.

On a personal note, having served my time as an inductee and now a complier of such anthologies, I can understand the appeal of these grouped introductions of younger poets (Ireland's own recent *Queering the Green* anthology was an excellent example of the genre), since there feels something especially exciting about reading the early writings of a good poet.

We hear that magic in a line (such as Michael Grieve's "Love sees the undeserving man, and serves.") or read the elegant and unexpected turn in the image (as in Roshni Gallagher's "In our house, the sound of the water// was silent as a bird lifting/ from a distant English field") or the sheer violence of the music (Colin Bramwell "Bit iver since yir luve wis tint,/ yir licht's jist naa the same.") and isn't there the sense that the poets, given a fair wind, could end up anywhere.

Niall Campbell is a poet from the Outer Hebrides of Scotland. His first poetry collection, Moontide *(2014), was published by Bloodaxe Books and won the Edwin Morgan Poetry Award and the Saltire First Book of the Year.* Noctuary *(2019), his second collection, was shortlisted for the Forward Prize for Best Collection. His latest collection,* The Island in the Sound *(Bloodaxe) was published in 2024. He is the Poetry Editor of* Poetry London *and lives in Newport on Tay, Fife.*

WHEN I SEE THE STARS IN THE NIGHT SKY

Marjorie Lotfi

I feel the sharp edge of Perspex on my palm,
the sixth-grade project, how I plotted them
    across a plastic arc to map out the dark.
A week of after-school hours hunched
    over books and charts, inscribing names
but mostly calculating the angles between
    them, how we know Orion by his belt,
how dipper's edge points to North Star.
    When it was done, I carried it out to
our tiny back yard, its brown slatted fence
    holding off the city street. I lifted my work
against the points of light to check that it was
    right, then rushed back into the warmth.

Marjorie Lofti was born in 1971 in New Orleans. She is an Iranian-American and grew up in Tehran. She holds a BA in English, a JD Law and an MSC in Creative Writing. She is the author of The Wrong Person to Ask *(Bloodaxe Books, 2023), which won the 2024 Forward Prize for Best First Collection. It was also shortlisted for the Saltire Prize for Best Book of Poetry and was one of the winners of the inaugural James Berry Prize and a Poetry Book Society Special Commendation. Her previous pamphlets are* The World May Be The Same *(Stewed Rhubarb, 2023) and* Refuge *(Tapsalteerie Press, 2018). She is the Co-Founder and Director of Open Book, a freelance writer, and a Royal Literary Fund Fellow. She divides her time between Edinburgh and Galloway.*

KAIETEUR FALLS

Roshni Gallagher

The waterfall hung in the landing
like a gesture. I passed it every day
and every day, the painting frothed
in the light of the window.

Golden Potaro River. Dense rainforest
green as stained glass. The shadows
of many animals moving.
In our house, the sound of the water

was silent as a bird lifting
from a distant English field.
Silent as memory shifting within
my grandparents – looking with all its eyes.

Sometimes it seems the water runs thin
as sugarcane, as the winding paths
that coil wetly around gold pits,
as the seam of minerals in rock.

Sometimes I'm shrouded in mist
as water plummets beneath me
and carves an opening through
the years into the cliff.

Rasni Gallagher was born in Leeds in 1997. She has an MA in English and History from the University of Edinburgh. Her pamphlet Cherry Bird *was published by Verve Poetry Press in 2023. She was a winner of the 2022 Edwin Morgan Poetry Award and awarded a 2022 Scottish Book Trust New Writers Award. She lives in Edinburgh.*

AUTUMN GEESE AT MONTROSE BASIN

Taylor Strickland

for Steve Byrne

The pinkfoots herald winter.
September's loudest thousands.
To witness their wild arrival and
find yourself likewise, winged
arms thrown out as you soar, fly
towards the edge of the world
that has no edge, these small miles
Scotland steals from the North
Sea, and you from the pinkfoots
returning anew in wink-wink
migrations, daybreak breached
after braving the hard arctic, freak
jet stream oscillations and thin air
thinning, and all for the promise
of rest, of mudflats and fields
of scythed oats. So the pear pitted
splits apart. So the blossom-loss.
Last year's frosts did them in but
whatever our past failure, listen.
The geese sing still. Just listen.

Taylor Strickland was born in Tallahassee, Florida in 1984. He has a BA, MLitt, and PhD. His book of translations of Alasdair Mac Mhaighstir Alasdair, Dastram/Delirium, *was published in 2024 and his pamphlet of his own poems,* Commonplace Book, *was published in 2022, both with Broken Sleep Books. He teaches occasionally at University of Glasgow, Islay and Borders Book Festivals and Glasgow Cathedral Festival. He lives in Glasgow.*

DEFENCE OF THE REALM

Sam Tongue

This is not a territory we can all inhabit;
a steepled hillside above the village, May
advancing slowly upwards in green, white, yellow,
garlicky blooms and a dead badger laid into its grassy bed
with no sign of struggle, as if thrown out of paradise.
I am breathless in this ambient untimeliness
and wild suspicion, a tug of waxwool snagged
on the wire and the war grinds on
in the valleys and the cowsheds, the rough fields
unrolling like beach matting. The badger is a lonely casualty
up here amongst the cairn-stones and salt-licks:
such baby-fine hair; that prize-fighter's grin; a gift
of bone structure and claw, freshly dead
on a bellyful of sweet pheasant eggs,
wild thyme subtle on the nose.

Samuel Tongue was born in Bath in 1981. He took a BA and MA at University of Exeter and a PhD at University of Glasgow. He is author of one poetry collection, Sacrifice Zones *(Red Squirrel, 2020) and three pamphlets:* The Nakedness of the Fathers *(Broken Sleep, 2022),* Stitch *(Tapsalteerie, 2018) and* Hauling-Out *(Eyewear, 2016). He was a winner of a New Writers Award from the Scottish Book Trust and is currently working as the Project Coordinator at the Scottish Poetry Library. He lives in Glasgow.*

JOHN KNOX, DYING

Michael Grieve

Remarkably, it was a peaceful going.
That such a body slipped beyond the scrim
of scripture spoken by his gathered friends
in such a hush may be a form of justice.
His pulpit bark demanded discipline,
discipleship from every human creature,
and lectured the elect with vulgar zeal.

At the eleventh hour he raised a hand
as sign that he should shed the vanity
of life in favour of the promise he
had nearly and yet never offered forth:
that desperate men are saved despite themselves.
Love sees the undeserving man, and serves.

Michael Grieve was born in Kirkcaldy in 1994. He has an MA in English from the University of St Andrews and an MPhil from the University of Cambridge. His pamphlet Luck *was published by HappenStance in 2018. He is currently a high school English teacher and lives in Ladybank.*

DELHI, NIGHT

Medha Singh

Congeries of impossibility–
        imagine a love up there
a vortex is hotting up;
        here, warmth, arriving
in the quiet cold.

Temple bells muting their clangour
     the glass factory done slowly blinding
its rubber slippered workers
       and the Muezzin
squarely asleep.

A dog doused in the moonlight
     is swatting flies in the orange light
with its mud-robed paw.

Medha Singh is a poet and translator based in Edinburgh.

MARICRUZ PAREDES

Colin Bramwell

Eftir Parra, y para mi suegra

Waulkin throu the oors ae gowd,
hame is whaur ye've led us.
Bit whaur is it yir gangin noo,
Maricruz Paredes?

A year's a lang time no tae wark,
I wonder hou yir heid is.
I wonder hou ye find the wards,
Maricruz Paredes?

They faa fae ye like rain—
cochino, apareces—
ye're cryin some poor saul a grumphie,
Maricruz Paredes?

If anely I cud ken
jist whit that ither ward ye said wiss.
Whun ye speak the tide gangs in,
Maricruz Paredes.

Aa yir wards brak ower my heid
wae a stour's insistence.
I won't forget ye, Mhairi-Sea,
bit yir in the distance.

Come visit us in Europe,
wull shaw ye whaur the Med is.
Thirs a coast as warm as yirs,
Maricruz Paredes.

Later, fae the seicont flair,
soondae clashmaclaivers.
Yir talkin trash aboot yir son
and aa his saicret lovers.

Wance ye were a daughter,
mony nichts confeerin
tae the sicht ae daw
as throu a skylicht peerin.

Bit iver since yir luve wis tint,
yir licht's jist naa the same.
Ivry time the sun gangs doun
it faas fae ye like rain,

til ye switch that lamp aff
jist neist tae whaur yir bed is.
Sleep noo in the eftirglaw,
Maricruz Paredes.

gangin – going | cochino – pig (used as an insult) | apareces – you appear | saul – soul | grumphie – pig | stour – storm | seicont flair – second floor | clashmaclaivers – gossip | confeerin – comparing | daw – dawn

See biographical note on p 36.

"YOU HAD A DAUGHTER. I FEEL SAD FOR HER."

Nuala Watt

Before I can find
    Don't touch her!
she has your hair
        and is gone –
before I can leave
disbelief
    the ruffle is over.

Does she think
    I have given you
      squintness?
        That your glowing
ride on my walking frame
is a necessity
    and not a treat?

I wish she were part of the haar,
part of the gloaming,
    a play-shiver learnt
from folktales.
    Ripped
from a fairy hill,
    not from our street.

You shake off one more burst
of adult strangeness
     but she has made me
a seabird clogged
      with corrosive sorrow.
You still want
   to go to the stories.
      I want to go home.

Nuala Watt was born in Glasgow in 1984. She has an M.Litt in Creative Writing from St Andrews and, in 2015, obtained a PhD, entitled "Partial Sight, Dependency and Open Poetic Form", from the University of Glasgow. Her first poetry collection is The Department of Work and Pensions Assesses a Jade Fish *(Blue Diode Press, 2024), which was shortlisted for for the Saltire Society First Book of the Year Award. Her current interests include the relationship between partial sight and creative practice, disabled parenthood, disability representation in literature and welfare activism.*

THE RINGING STONE
Isle of Tiree

Tarn MacArthur

Sat like a fat thumb on the shoreline, this granite erratic
deposited on Lewisian gneiss. A boulder out of place
and time, whose Neolithic marks inform another sphere
we have no meaning for. Still, we go. And have come
to like it more for how its enigmatic faces soon resolve
into something like our own. Struck, it sounds a lone
note that echoes internally from an unfathomed source.
Like the heart's muted chorus. All significance made
palpable the moment it stops. Forgotten egg of the gods.
Its cold and flameless decay smoulders imperceptibly.
We knock and knock again. Receive the same response.
As if an answer could accommodate our appetite for loss.
When we fear we're forsaken we put an ear to the stone
and know it for its silence. Listen, there is comfort in this.

Tarn Painter-MacArthur was born in Montréal in 1986. He has a PhD in English Literature from the University of St Andrews and an MFA in Creative Writing from the University of Oregon. Recent poems have appeared in The New Republic, New Statesman, Poetry Review *and* Poetry London. *He is in the process of finishing his debut poetry collection. He recently received a research grant from Creative Scotland for a project exploring his family history on the Isle of Tiree and the archipelago of St Kilda. He currently lives in Edinburgh.*

SALVAGING

Tim Tim Cheng

In sunshowered Orkney, rainbows sprouted after I failed to withdraw cash. What a thing. To spend all my money to be in nature. To be in nature when I could not drive. According to the tour guide, *a boy once saw a soldier jump from a ship. From afar, the boy thought: that seems fun. I wanna join him.* Oil spilt along ice shards. Frozen water burned. Causes of death did not offset each other — as such, I found myself replying to emails after encircling the Ring of Brodgar, wind-bitten moss sandwiches. The circles were complete. Back on the tour bus, an upturned ladybug struggled. *One had to turn shipwrecks upside down to dispatch them from town to town. They were rumoured, too, to have been reused for satellites.* From sea to space, their ageless steel orbited our moonlit purposes. I sat with opposites, an empty seat, and looked out.

Tim Tim Cheng (she/they) was born in Hong Kong in 1993. She has an MSc in Creative Writing (Poetry) from the University of Edinburgh. The Tattoo Collector *(Nine Arches, 2024) was a Poetry Book Society Winter Recommendation.* Tapping at Glass *(Verve, 2023) was one of Poetry Society Books of the Year. They were one of the editors of* Where Else: An International Hong Kong Poetry Anthology *(Verve, 2023). She is currently working on a poetry-film, a hybrid book titled* Tongues on Rocks *and a Cantonese podcast on Anglophone poetry. They currently live in Glasgow.*

IF I COULDN'T SLEEP IN THE GRANARY
Agaete, 2023

Patrick Romero McCafferty

it's just because the walls were ghosting me
when I'd come all that way to hear them talk:
no here once lived & died; no knowledge gained
of fathers hiding from their daughters' love;
no ribald song or scream upon the draught,
my uneventful night not just unjust
but amping up my bargaining & threats
"spider, show me; mother, give me thistle —
arm me; give me, god, my thin web tongue"
moondrunk, everywhere at war but here,
I begged the settled dust for honest words,
a sign of each mistake made in that hollow
where they'd kept the grain for times of need
of which there must have once been tonnes & tonnes.

Patrick Romero McCafferty was born in Edinburgh in 1995. His debut pamphlet is forthcoming with ignitionpress in 2025. He currently works convening a program of creative writing workshops for young people. He continues to live in Edinburgh.

FIELDNOTES IN LAKE DISTRICT MIST

Alycia Pirmohamed

Tall trunks, gaps of sunlight, obscurity. Leaves on the
        path disassemble in the breeze /
In the breeze, ferns lift and glisten with rain. Light falls
        through the fell's ridge /
Light falls through the shape of leaves knitted together
        like hands in prayer /
Elongated. Reaching. Bare almost-winter arms /
She exits the stone formation and enters a new season.
        Water breaking at her ankles /
An invitation. A reincarnation. Her figure is a slippery
        mist of its own /

        Watch as she glides into a cluster of trees

Alycia Pirmohamed is a Canadian-born poet based in Scotland. She is the author of the poetry collection Another Way to Split Water. *In 2023, she won the Nan Shepherd Prize for her nonfiction debut* A Beautiful and Vital Place, *forthcoming from Canongate.*

DID YOU ALWAYS HAVE A PASSION FOR STAYING VERY STILL?
Questions I have for living statues

Iona Lee

What is the cruellest thing that a child has ever said to you?
Is there a restless mind within that slow breathing body, or
does being zen come with the territory? Would you describe
yourself as a patient person? What does it feel like to watch
a day pass by: the sun's slow progress; the disarray of crowds?
How do you not get distracted? Is that something
that you have to practice? And how do you decide
when it is time to end your shift? Does your act have a finale?
The living statue, departing the square. Can we perform
when there is no audience?

Iona Lee was born in Edinburgh in 1996. She has a BA in illustration from Glasgow School of Art and an MFA in Art and Humanities from Duncan of Jordanstone College of Art and Design. Her debut poetry collection Anamnesis *(Polygon, 2023) was shortlisted for the Edwin Morgan Award and won the Somerset Maugham Award. She works as a poet, illustrator and performer. She lives in Edinburgh.*

VENERY, OFF RANGE ROAD 134, EAST OF VEGREVILLE, ALBERTA

―

Patrick James Errington

Autumn, the air its fleshing knife.
The long hours drawn out, scraped

bare. What remains is quarry, hunched
and low, electric with cold – aspen, pine,

the long rushes raw in the low light, livid
as stripped wire.   Here, to move is

as a blade moves
                    across skin.
Frost alone stoops

to its Ayrshire needlework, its thread,
its suture. I watch, holding my breath

as though it were bird, or bullet, my shadow
stretching out into the undergrowth, a snare

-line shuddering then snapped taught, some
small and feral thing twisting at one end.

Patrick James Errington was born in Red Deer, Canada in 1989. He took a BA at the University of Alberta, an MFA at Columbia University and a PhD at the University of St Andrews. His poetry collection the swailing *(McGill-Queens University Press, 2023) was shortlisted for Scottish Poetry Book of the Year in the Saltire Scottish National Book Awards and won the John Pollard Foundation International Poetry Prize. His chapbooks are* Glean *(ignitionpress, 2018) and* Field Studies *(Clutag Press, 2019). He has also translated into French PJ Harvey's* The Hollow of the Hand *(Âge d'Homme, 2017). He is a Lecturer in Creative Writing and interdisciplinary researcher at the University of Edinburgh. He is currently translating philosopher E.M. Cioran's* Cahiers *for New York Review Books. He was the winner of the Bronwen Wallace Award from the Writers' Trust of Canada, the Callan Gordon Award from the Scottish Book Trust, the Poetry International Prize, the London Magazine Poetry Competition and the Wigtown Poetry Competition.*

DEATH TO MY HOMETOWN

Harry Ledgerwood

When at midday
they dragged   the detractors
through the high street –
with the lying folks
just lying   there,
              to be gawked at,
grabbing at swollen ankles
– he took off
       to the windmills,
chasing loose change and missing mothers.

When   at midnight
they lashed the widows   along the promenade
of seagulls squealing for sea dog days
and fishing myths.   Cries   made of tar
heard in the caravans   at dark
       came from the mottled lips of playparks

under the careful   eye of the constellation
shaped   like a gull
carrying the citizen's bag, stained
            by his belt of blood.

DEATH TO MY HOMETOWN

When at sunrise
                they robbed the pockets
of the bodies   sprawled
across the pitches,
           with the red glint
illuminating their spurting wounds,
he   stood at the hilltop
overlooking the Caledonia
he had never noticed before
                and yelled
again.   And the gull,
      bending his beak
towards the sea
dropped the bag from that great height.

Harry Ledgerwood is a poet and fiction writer from Ayr. His work has been published in The Oxford Review Of Books, Gutter Magazine, *and an anthology with the Hampden Collection. He was shortlisted for the Dart Prize and the Jon Stallworthy Prize.*

SWALLOWING THE ANCHOR

Siún Carden

The public hall's breezeblock walls
are Blu-Tacked with photos of young men
bare-chested or gansied, cuddling penguins
or flensing whales, gory to the oxters,
on a Kodachrome South Georgia pier.
Grey now, with wives and plates of fancies,
those men drain the tea urn, as their illicit still
above a work camp wardrobe glimmers down.
One wrote these captions, stuck above the buns

    CAPE PIGEONS FEEDING
    ON THE CLOTTED BLOOD

as if to shout that swallowing the anchor
doesn't stop it falling. The weight of one place,
once you take it in. A distance growing as it sinks.

Siún Carden is from County Down and lives in Shetland. She won a New Writers Award for poetry from the Scottish Book Trust in 2024. Her pamphlet Tract *was published by* The Well Review *in 2023. Some of her poems have appeared in* Magma, The Interpreter's House, The Glasgow Review of Books, Northwords Now *and* The New Shetlander, *as well as the anthologies* Almarks *(Culture Matters) and* The Middle of a Sentence *(The Common Breath).*

from ACTS OF JOY

Will Barnard

The scent of candlelight
and Rioja wine
The time we almost died
climbing Ben Nevis
The shape of granite
buttered into the skin
on my hands
The pull of a cigarette
after quitting
Weighted blankets
Soft clothes
The burn of sour sweets
and the lemon fumes
rising like workers from bed
from a fresh mop
The pastry counter
Heartache
and gambling
Rows and rows of bread
in the shop
and don't you just want
to squeeze it?

Will Barnard lives and works in Glasgow, has been published in Poetry London, *and won an Eric Gregory Award in 2024.*

A SOUNDING BOX

FORKIT TONGUE

Brian Holton

Heave awa lads, we're no deid yit!

"When my grandmother makes a mistake, she says 'Ah tell a leh'...
But I feel the same whenever I use conversational English picked
up after fourteen years at Oxford. Or whenever I lapse into a full-
throated Dundonian Scots at home and someone announces, 'Ye've
no lost yir accent'. Herbert speak with forked tongue."

(WN Herbert *Forked Tongue*, in Brown C.,
Paterson, D. eds. *Don't Ask Me What I Mean*, 2003)

Ay, me tae, Bill. This feeling of not being entirely at home in either the majority or the minority language is common among speakers of smaller languages, and I have heard similar feelings expressed by speakers of Tibetan and other ethnic minority languages in China, as well as by speakers of the half-dozen Chinese languages that are as different from Mandarin as French is from Portuguese. Indeed, in Montreal some years ago, a member of the staff at the Kahnawà:ke Education Center, a teacher of the Mohawk language, said to me in astonishment during a discussion of minority languages in Europe, "I never knew white people had the same problem we do". Div oo no juist!

Scotland is a nation with three languages and literatures. (Gaelic, Scots, and English, though there is also a considerable corpus of work in Latin: see for instance Robert Crawford, *Apollos of the North: Selected Poems of George Buchanan and Arthur Johnston*, 2006.) It's important to remember that the English language is not indigenous to Scotland, having been introduced in the mid-16th century with the circulation of the Geneva Bible in English during the years leading up to and encompassing the Reformation. Gaelic is of course, indigenous, and before the introduction of the northern dialect of Old English from Northumbria in the 8th century, it was the language of prestige throughout Scotland, as the tongue of kings and courts, and was only supplanted by Scots in the 14th century at court; Latin was the language of church, parliament and law until supplanted by Scots at the same time.

Scots is a West Germanic language with a literature going back more than 800 years, yet Scotland is a country where only English is compulsory in schools, where Scotland's history is barely taught beyond primary school, and where (non-Scottish) newspaper owners have been known to prohibit the reviewing of Scottish books on the grounds that this would be "provincial", while the myopic hegemony of the Anglocentric media enshrines a set of attitudes which routinely ignores or belittles our culture. (See Emma Gibbs, *Brora, the best British beach you've never heard of*, *The Guardian* 6.9.2023: who is "you" here? Is the sub-editor assuming that 5.6 million Scots have never heard of Brora? Or that no one – of any importance – lives there.)

And too many Scots are complicit in this, from the "Yes, but…" of civil servants and politicians that the late Aonghas MacNeacail described (*Rage Against the Dying Of… Chapman* 35-6, 1983), to those Scotch cringers whose union-jackery masks a deep denial of and distaste for the culture they grew up in. And there are still ignorant politicians and ill-informed teachers untrained in linguistics pronouncing that Scots is not a language in its own right, but *Bad English*, *Lazy Speech*, or *Slang*: they are wrong, every last one of them.

However, social media has now made possible the spread of a vigorous Cyber-Scots in all its wild variety, from Shetland to Donegal and every airt between. More books in Scots are being published every year, and at the time of writing a Scottish Languages Bill is making its way through the Scottish Parliament in Edinburgh: this, it is hoped, will at the very least give Scots the same resources and support which is currently given to Gaelic, which might ideally include a TV channel and local and national radio stations. However, if intensive teacher training is not part of the process, the Scots tongue will still be struggling, for teacher training is a long slow process, involving as it does the long effort to help existing teachers unlearn the prejudices they inherited from their teachers. Progress will occur funeral by funeral, no doubt, as the old bigotries and ignorance wither and die.

Heave awa lads, we're no deid yit!

I learned my Scots from my mother's family. Her father Samuel McDiarmid Young, a policeman's son, had a remarkable career: apprenticed to a blacksmith in Duns, the Army took him to France in WWI and turned him into a mechanical engineer who serviced and drove the buses taking soldiers to the front line; later he was driver to an officer in the army of occupation in

Cologne, and after leaving the army, sold army-surplus engines to the fishermen on the Berwickshire coast and installed them on their Fifie and Zulu sailing boats, then became the main Scottish dealer for Packard and Reo, had a car showroom in Edinburgh, and ran small fast buses between Edinburgh and Peebles until he was bought out by William Alexander (of the famous coachbuilding works in Falkirk), who was then running a competing service.

Previously, in Cologne in 1919, after Sam had made a reputation as a performer in camp concerts in France, singing and impersonating Charlie Chaplin, his officer heard him sing and took him to the opera house, which changed his life. After selling his businesses he took voice lessons from Alastair Sim, and sang for a couple of seasons with the Scottish Grand Opera Society, the precursor of Scottish Opera: "Abnormal", was how Sim described Sam's light tenor voice – even in his fifties, he could hit high notes that Gigli and Caruso strained to reach. In the 1930s he became a market gardener and trade union organiser, then after WWII he went to Heriot-Watt College (as it then was), graduating with a BSc in electrical engineering, and was in charge of Falkirk power station when he retired.

Sailing for the first time to France as a soldier, he couldn't keep his food down and had lost his appetite, so he told a medical officer, "Doctor, A cannae tak ma mait": the doctor, not being a Scots speaker, didn't know *mait* is the equivalent of English *food*, so put him on a vegetarian diet.

One of his favourite stories was about a Border family that moved to Edinburgh: their daughter had been sternly told she had to speak proper, so when someone came to the door asking for her father, she replied "Faither's in the gairding, howking ding".

His wife, my granny, Christina Cunningham Rae, daughter of a craftsman in a Galashiels tweed mill, was a darner in the mill before marriage, and thereafter a housewife, so never had to acquire spoken English for purposes of work. Chrissy had a big repertoire of bairn-rhymes and tales, like *Peggy wi the Gowden Leggie*, which told how a wicked girl killed her sister and stole her golden leg, and her sister's ghost haunted her, standing by her bed in the dark chanting "Peggy, Peggy, A want ma gowden leggie", until she died of fright. From that story, her awful warning to a bairn that pauchled a biscuit or told a lie was, "Mind, eer haun'll wag, an the craws'll come an pyke at it".

As a teenager in the Border folk clubs of the '60s, I immersed myself in the world of the classic ballads – some of which I still sing – and the ballad stanza can be glimpsed beneath many of my Scots translations of classical Chinese poetry. Furthermore, it is impossible to understate the contribution Robert

Burns made to the preservation and continuation of the unbroken tradition of Scots song: he spent the last years of his life collecting songs for Johnson's *Scots Musical Museum* and other collections, and his songs and poems were an early and profound influence on me. The Scots verse of Hugh McDiarmid knocked me sideways when I first read it as a teenager: it changed my life for ever, and led me to the work I do today.

At Galashiels Academy in the 1960s, Donald MacInnes taught us to read Scots by including Scots literature in the Higher English syllabus, so we read everything from the Makars to McDiarmid and beyond: this may have been the only secondary school in Scotland at the time where Scots was taught so widely.

———

Sae, forkit tongues? Whaur div oo gaun fae here? Border bairns dinnae hear or see Scots on the Internet, tho they'll mebbes text the wey they speak. The're some grand wark bein dune bi fowk like the Scots Language Centre an the Dictionars o the Scots Leid (baith fundit bi the Scottish Government), an yin or twae MSPs tak an interest, but it's aye a sair fecht to get heard. An whit for did I scrieve this piece in the English an no in the Scots?

A'll sae't again: Heave awa lads, we're no deid yit!

Brian Holton, born in Galashiels in 1949, and educated at the Universities of Edinburgh and Durham, has published more than twenty books and pamphlets of translated poetry, including Yang Lian's Venice Elegy *(Edizioni Damocle, 2019) and* Narrative Poem *(Bloodaxe Books, 2017). In 2021, he was awarded the inaugural Sarah McGuire Prize for Poetry Translation for Yang Lian's* Anniversary Snow *(Shearsman Books, 2019). Holton's collection of classical poems in Scots,* Staunin Ma Lane, *was published by Shearsman Books in 2016, and his* Hard Roads an Cauld Hairst Winds: Li Bai an Du Fu in Scots *by Taproot Press in early 2022.* Hard Roads an Cauld Hairst Winds *was nominated for Scots Book of the Year, Scots Language Awards 2022. His latest book of translations from the Classical Chinese,* Aa Cled Wi Clouds She Cam: 60 Lyrics frae the Chinese *(Translations in Scots and English), was published by The Irish Pages Press in 2022.*

He has won other prizes both for his own poetry in Scots and for his translations into both Scots and English. He is a recovering academic who taught Chinese language and literature at Edinburgh, Durham and Newcastle, and translation at Newcastle and the Hong Kong Polytechnic University. He has given lectures, readings and workshops at universities and major literary festivals in the UK, Spain, Italy, Holland, New Zealand, China, the USA, and Canada. He lives in Melrose in the Scottish Borders, close to where he was born.

CLEACHDADH AN NEACH-CHIÙIL

Niall O'Gallagher

Anns a' mhadainn, togaidh mi an fhìdheall
bhon a' bhogsa, teannachadh a' bhogha
a chuireas mi sìos taobh thall na drochaid.
Uair eile, tionndaidhidh mi gach iuchair,
a' cur mo chlaisneachd ri fonn nan teudan
gus dearbhadh gu bheil an uirlis gleusta.

Is doirbh ceòl a chumadh a tha gleusta
don chuisle, don chorn air neo don fhìdheill,
do choisir nan glòr no buidhinn teudan,
don cheòl-fhoireann, nan suidh' ann am bogha
air neo do phiàna mòr nan iuchar
a chumas sinn sùil air thar nan drochaid.

Oir feumar fonn a cheangladh le drochaid
agus iad a' gluasad tro na gleusan,
gach pàirt a sgrìobhadh a rèir a h-iuchrach
fhèin: an tè thrìobailte do na fidhlean
a-mhàin am measg na chleachdas am bogha
gus an ceòl a tharraing bho na teudan.

Coiseachd air tost mar chleasaiche teuda
eadar dà bhalla far nach eil drochaid,
ga chumail teann gus nach dèan e bogha:
saoileam gur e sin an dòigh as gleusta
air a mhìneachadh – togail na fidhle,
ionnsramaid le dà ghlais ach gun iuchair

gus am fosgladh. Oir chan eil aon iuchair
eil' ach cleachdadh a bheir air na teudan
gàire dhomhain mar nach ann air fìdheill
daonna bha iad sìnte; chan eil drochaid
eile dh'ionnsaigh ciùil a tha cho gleusta
's gun sàth e cridhe mar shaigheid bhogha.

Mar sin, togaidh mi uair eil' am bogha,
m' òrdag cho dlùth anns an eig mar iuchair
ann an toll, feuchainn a bheil i gleusta
lem làimh chlì mus bean ròineach ri teudan,
deiseil airson seinn. 'S e ceòl an drochaid
a bheir sinn thar aisling fiodha fìdhle.

'S ann mar bhogha tha tonn fuaim nan teudan,
na iuchar don chridhe, faileas drochaid
thar aibhne, air ghleus le ceòl na fìdhle.

Niall O'Gallagher is the author of three collections of poetry in Gaelic published by Clàr. A verse-novella, Litrichean Plàighe, *and a novella in prose for children are in preparation. His selected poems,* Fuaimean Gràidh / The Sounds of Love, *with English translations by Peter Mackay, Deborah Moffatt and others, was published by Francis Boutle in 2023. A translator from Catalan, he is currently Gaelic Writer in Residence at the University of Edinburgh. Niall lives on the west coast of Scotland with his wife and their two children.*

TWO DIPTYCHS

David Kinloch

In the folds of life.

FOLD

The childhood pastime I was most invested in was an origami game called "fortune teller", though it goes by other names as well. I was fascinated by the range of different fates my little fingers could generate just by folding paper and then making it flower again to reveal stories. And when I see my childhood self I see a creature folded over like that "cootie catcher", as others called it, all angles and secret words, my core held from beneath like an ice cream cone.

I liked the idea that here was a truth about myself, or a riddle, and it was inscrutable perhaps even when revealed by the process of unfolding. But there are some truths that virgin paper is too frail to hold or conjure and as the years pass the pressure grows and grows until you have to unfold yourself, smooth out your creases and show yourself to the world.

The origami dream world never leaves you though. That sense of a privacy teased but protected, a rice paper intimacy that is essentially "you" and for you and in offering it you violate yourself just a little, tarnish that sense of soul.

According to the great German philosopher, Gottfied Leibnitz, however, the self is an affair of two storeys, an upper room where the soul resides and a lower material chamber. Both are shaped by labyrinths of folds and coils and one of our tasks as human beings is to discover how to bring these baroque folds into communication with each other. He deploys the image of veins of marble to both in different contexts; sometimes the veins are twisted coils of matter caught in the stone, so that a block of marble is like an undulating loch full of fish. Sometimes the veins are innate ideas in the soul which fankle with the suspended energy of potential statues caught in a block of marble. Matter is marbled, and the soul is marbled, in two different ways. Descartes was limited by his rather prim insistence on the world of straight lines. But Leibnitz saw curves and whorls everywhere and that the human body and soul were caught up in them even at the level of the microscopic monad.

Like most teenagers I knew there was a cauldron of matter bubbling up from below but as I grew older I realised that I needed to connect it or bring it into alignment with the technical, musical folds I was developing little by little in that occluded upper chamber; a space that needed the views, the opinions, the rage, the humiliation I could so clearly distinguish from the windows of the lower room. Leibnitz speaks of the upper chamber as "a sounding box" which would allow you to hear the visible motion coming from below stairs. Suddenly then, there is poetry itself, a sounding box rustling with the folded silks of matter. But it must be opened, it must be viewed and heard; it must be unfolded and for that you need time, a place, people who might bend towards you as you bend towards them. Then a new game of whispers might begin.

I didn't want to "confess" anything though. It was more a question of "disclosure". "Confession" has its roots in the religious admission of sin or guilt but "disclosure" is upbeat and quite free of such connotations. One online dictionary presents a definition of disclosure dating from the 1590s: " an act of opening up to view, a making known or revealing". So the poetry in which I eventually discovered a "voice", or something approaching, and articulated a nascent gay identity was a conscious speaking out, a creature of daylight that actively resisted – even though it might describe or evoke – any sense of shame that society attached to it.

But in those very early days what was it precisely that I wanted to share? At the start it could not really be "poetry" even if I called it that. Perhaps just the simple fact of "me"; the fold in the universe that seemed to be me. A disclosure, rather than a confession. Not out of solipsism – perhaps – but out of fear that this specific instance of being that the universe had taken might never be noticed because, in the main, the universe kept folding away from me, trundling off on familiar rails to places it seemed to be more comfortable with. Of course much of this was just a variation on teenage angst. But what has remained from this prologue is that when I stand up to read my poetry in public I rarely feel that I am simply offering poetry. *I* am there, a person in body and soul and I fold up this way, not that way, and I'd like to share this fold in the universe with you. Not *because of me* though but because it shows the *world* in a slightly different aspect. Each reading is a performance of a self's encapsulation of the world caught up in language. That performance contains its shreds and patches of convenient fiction but it may also allow a glimpse of what is unique and what can be extracted from the fold that is you. So the poetry reading never feels like the ephemeral event it is sometimes taken to be but is almost vascular in nature, the disclosure of specific veins running through the marbled fabric of the world. How much of this, however, is mere wishful thinking, an evanescent rainbow that seems to bend towards us?

There is a painting that expresses this peculiar mixture of intimacy and disclosure very well. It's by the French Renaissance artist Jean Fouquet and depicts the Virgin Mary getting ready to breastfeed the infant Jesus; a work that the modern world can understand intellectually but which it probably struggles with at an emotional level. It's not the imminent breastfeeding that is difficult but how the other actors in the scene conduct themselves. It's known as *The Melun Diptych* although the two panels making up the painting hang in different galleries. Occasionally, however, the two halves are brought together and the artist's intentions become more clear. On the left hand panel we see a depiction of the man who commissioned the work, Etienne Chevalier. He stands dressed in an expensive red coat, his hands clasped together in prayerful adoration as he contemplates the Virgin and Child represented in the right hand panel. Standing beside Chevalier is the much taller, angular figure of Saint Stephen who bears in his hands one of the stones used to martyr him. One of the many peculiarities of this painting, this stone resembles a meteorite and has been identified successfully by scholars as exactly that. A heavenly stoning indeed. There is much that is weird about this painting that requires careful decoding: Chevalier's skin is dark brown in hue but his praying hands are completely white; Chevalier and Saint Stephen are realistically depicted but the Virgin is an extraordinary creature, her flesh a snowy white like that of her son's. That this is meant to symbolise the holy couple's purity goes without saying but is the Virgin sitting on her throne or standing or in the process of getting up? One of her breasts is demurely covered but the other, which forms a perfect globe, is completely bare and the distance between said breasts is anatomically suspect to say the least. Even Olympic athletes would struggle to achieve so broad a chest. Many scholars have laboured to propose ingenious interpretations but one in particular, Monja Schünemann, may have cracked the code. She has asked us to consider that, originally, this work of art had a hinge. This painting, in fact, is a fold and depends for its meaning on the performative opening and closing of the two panels. It depends, in other words on the action of the spectator who is more than a spectator but an actor in the drama whose intimate touch gives birth to the painting in all its aspects.

When the left hand panel is closed over to meet the right we discover – thanks to infrared reflectography – that the positioning of the characters in the painting is very carefully calculated and the Virgin's slightly awkward pose and anatomy clarified. As Chevalier folds towards the Virgin his lips approach her lactating breast and the Christ child's pointing hand indicates the location of Chevalier's heart. His head completely obscures the Virgin's naked breast thus making accusations of prurience less likely. As a whole the painting is an extraordinary variation on a genre known as a "lactation"; it is similar to a palimpsest but not exactly that, an early form of installation or performance art where intimacy and disclosure are balanced across the fold encouraged by the painting's hinge. It is both delicate and bold at the same time, both witholding and expressive. When the diptych is open, the characters seem almost to bend or incline slightly towards each other, on the brink of action; the final moment of disclosure, of faith, however is too intimate to be gazed upon. You can see this only with the eyes of the soul, or of the imagination, simultaneously visible and invisible. We might even see it as a graphic illustration of Leibnitz's later images of how the folds of being communicate between the monad's lower and upper storeys.

These delicate games of hide and seek, this exploration of fold within fold, of what you can give of self and what you would prefer to withhold, were a kind of luxury that a modern American artist and writer David Wojnarowicz could not afford. Across the pond, while I was gingerly choreographing my twentysomething's self-disclosures, Wojnarowicz began work on a graphic memoir *7 Miles a Second* in collaboration with artists James Romberger and Marguerite Van Cook. Here he illustrates his early life as a teenage hustler in Manhattan, a homeless runaway and, latterly, AIDS activist in the front line of the struggle against the homophobic politics of the American government. This extraordinary "comic" prefers a kind of rigid juxtaposition of images to a baroque folding. Because – as today – his society was so profoundly fractured in its understandings of sexuality and how to live it out that absolutely no compromise was possible. His art works seem full of borders that might aspire to be hinges but you know instinctively when you look at them that they don't work this way, that no folding over to meet the other, to commune with them in an intimate pooling of self, will ever be possible. One panel in particular is instructive and could be viewed almost as the polar opposite of Fouquet's gentle acts of communion although – not so ironically – religious belief marks them both. The page is occupied by two linked but diametrically opposed images: a dark block of written text – an unpunctuated expression of Wojnarowicz's anger in the face of Cardinal Joseph O'Connor's abhorrent policies on AIDS – fills the extreme left hand margin. The rest of the page is taken up by a portrait of Wojnarowicz himself transformed into a terrifying giant slamming his fist down brutally on the spire of St Patrick's Cathedral. The moment of graphic violence completely dwarfs the written evocation of frustration and despair. As critic Rami Fawaz has suggested, words alone are not sufficient to encapsulate the enormity of the feelings provoked by institutional prejudice. But they act like a flare of ignition for the complementary visual image.

Both Fouquet and Wojnarowicz, however, seem to come from worlds where the self is forged out of a necessary certainty. In Fouquet's case that conferred by Christian belief and in Wojnarowicz's from the angry despair that creates oppositional identity. But the origami game that told my childhood fortune is known by different names even if it is played all over the world. For "cootie-catcher" is also "whirlybird" and "chatterbox", "pick-a-colour" and "bugcatcher". In French it is "le quatre coin" or "cocotte", "flip-flap" in Danish, "beak" in Icelandic, "Loppa" in Swedish, "Csiki ćsuki" in Hungarian. The names of the self we seek are as variegated as the veins in Leibnitz's marbled two storey house and which sometimes take some mysterious detours in their acts of communication. What I've come to understand – at first dimly and instinctively perhaps – is that catching the self, or the self's perception of the world, and expressing it effectively, is a mixture of construction and chance discovery. You fold the paper carefully but once the game is up and running any combination of colours and numbers and words seems possible. Where will you land? And it is so much more fun, the permutations so greatly enlarged when you play this game with friendly or even competitive others, the touch of their fold to yours as necessary as the shy revelation of your own intimate choices. One of the names of this origami game is "poem maker".

ANNUNCIATION

Annunciation is like a nighttime moth that swerves in from the solid dark; or the sudden realisation in a Tuscan field that a sea of fire flies have taken you as their pole star. It's the moment your foot pauses above a South Uist machair of flowers so jewel-like it can't risk injuring a single one.

Annunciation is intimate and involves a turning; not an Orphic turning. That's too mythopoetic for these fall days. But a turning over, a revolution even, although this hardly does justice to the incremental nature of the experience. Birth is not a sudden event but a gestation.

This is something the greatest painter of one of the most famous Biblical encounters seems to have understood instinctively or even, perhaps, by virtue of a supernatural grace.

The Archangel Gabriel drops in unannounced on the Virgin Mary to tell her she will bear a son. But most paintings of the Christian Annunciation seem to miss the essentially private character of that encounter. The glacial perfection of Da Vinci's fashion competition is set against a background of exquisitely topiaried trees. Nobody could quite believe the mannerist contortion of the Virgin as she twists away from the angel in Botticelli's version. Only the Dominican monk Fra Angelico gets it right in a painting that was conceived as installation art, animating many of the architectural features of the cloisters where he spent his life and actively but discreetly involving the spectator in the event depicted.

The shapes and colours of this work have a supernal clarity that gesture beyond its aspect towards the mysteries it incarnates and are typical of the finest Italian Renaissance paintings: one quarter of the canvas is reserved for a grieving Adam and Eve, apples at their feet, expelled from grassy, green Eden by an angel sitting on top of a tree. And then beneath a vaulted blue portico studded with stars, Gabriel inclines towards Mary, his hands clasped reverently across his chest. He is dressed mostly in pink although his wings, tough and tawny, scintillate because Angelico has included silica in the mix of paint. The seated Virgin, wrapped in her traditional blue cloak, mimics the angel's pose. A golden beam emerging from the hand of God cuts diagonally downwards across the image and the holy spirit in the form of a small rocket propelled dove complete with halo shoots down to touch her.

What is most striking about this beautiful but spare image, however, is the way the gaze of each of the two protagonists almost meets and sets up a dialogue between them. Indeed the entire work is plotted as a dramatisation of a fully embodied looking, for when you examine it closely you realise that the lines of perspective are so steep you have to kneel in order to view the painting properly. In fact it wasn't exactly supplication of this kind that Angelico sought to harness here. It seems, rather, that he wished instead to invoke the kinetic nature of annunciation, of gestation. Apparently, this painting was designed to be placed at the top of a long flight of stairs leading to the first floor of the monastery where the Dominican monks had their own individual cells. So, as they climbed, they ascended through Angelico's divine lines of sight, the entire scene emerging slowly into a perfect perspective, their own gaze seeking and meeting those of the painting's holy protagonists. At the top of the stairs they would pause and say the words of greeting and prayer "Ave Maria" before moving towards cells which were also decorated with images that they would then physically imitate in the process of their devotion.

Some commentators on this work have suggested that Mary looks directly back at Gabriel conveying a sense of selfhood and agency. In Luke's Gospel, when Mary receives the angel's news, it is said that "she was troubled at his saying, and cast about in her mind what manner of salutation this should be". Fra Angelico paints a supremely human moment before acceptance and acquiescence follows. But this is not fully accurate. Annunciation works via small, unexpected changes. In fact the Virgin looks slightly past the angel, an inward gaze filling her eyes as she seems to contemplate what has just been announced. Similarly, although the Dominican spectators raise their gaze to meet those of Gabriel and Mary they are drawn inevitably by the lines of perspective to the painting's true vanishing point made up of a little barred window at the back of the portico. This window and the touch of greenery behind can be read as both a continuation of the Garden of Eden which flourishes beside and beyond the portico and as a representation of the "hortus conclusus", the enclosed and inviolate garden that symbolises the Virgin's immaculate nature. In this way, the theologically instructed gaze seeks to interrogate a mystery that the power of paint, itself a form of incarnation, may only point towards. Such are the fruits of scholarship when combined with acts of patient looking.

Looking at, looking beyond and looking in, a process in which I've been actively engaged while trying to write these pieces but also to live and process through this part of my life. So it is that I see some of the acts of the earlier half of my existence through the prism of annunciation. God, as the cliché goes, is love. In a way, then, annunciation is the first act of that love, love's opening gambit. When I turned away – without much in the way of virginal contortion – from the protestant church of my childhood to become a Roman Catholic at the age of 25 I managed to convince myself of this equation. Hopelessly in love, I assumed God's presence at the heart of this love and bagged romance and religion in a double deal that thoroughly confused all the participants. The romance was a fantasy and the religion unable to take root in the version practised in South Wales where I was translated shortly after. At this point I reasoned that I should not have changed my religion but simply come out as gay. And I've maintained this rather banal explanation for the best part of thirty years, resolutely avoiding all things religious and severely critical of myself for choosing an affiliation so openly hostile to all varieties of sexual difference.

Carl Jung once stated "One cannot live the afternoon of life according to the programme of life's morning; for what was great in the morning will be of little importance in the evening, and what in the morning was true will at evening become a lie." Life as a diptych, then, a thing of two sometimes contradictory halves. But what if it were more complicated than that? What if the moment of annunciation was indeed mistaken but not quite in the way you have assumed all these many years? And that it is in the midst of this second panel of the diptych that a truer pattern announces itself? What happens when the waters in a waterfall of little events and experiences and encounters resolve into features you have met before? You are brought up short before an unexpected act of love, a declaration of profound friendship, say, and the circles of ramification it sets in motion. You realise you have been here, exactly here, before and are so shocked by that symmetry that you wonder if – just perhaps – an intention greater than your own has been playing out through the thirty plus years since the original events and that you should not have walked away from both the other players first time around. Or could it simply be the ever so predictable performance of your own deep-seated character content to reprise its role after all this time? So, like the Virgin, you are troubled, your gaze turns inward.

And when that happens you realise that you have not looked patiently enough. Yes, annunciation is often a personal, infinitesimal moment. A shower of leaves falling at your feet in autumn can be an annunciation; a mouse runs under the cooker when the light goes on; a lover who has been gazing shyly at the floor looks up and directly into your eyes. Suddenly then, it is clear that no-one has noticed one crucial detail in Fra Angelico's great painting. As the monks gazed up the stairway towards the painted drama their eyes were indeed drawn to the little window in the back wall but could they have noticed the tiny figure placed in the top left hand corner? They would have known about it from years of familiarity with the work but could they have actually seen it as they ascended? A figure observing the Annunciation and maybe looking back at them? Its identity is not certain. Is it a little bird flown in from Eden? A butterfly, perhaps, a psyche, symbol of the human soul? Or a smudge in the paint? It isn't visible in all the reproductions of the painting I've seen but in some surely it is present? Or is it simply present in my mind's eye, the incarnation of second thoughts?

We cast about in the solid but illuminated dark wondering what manner of salutation this could be, awaiting angel or moth.

David Kinloch was born and brought up in Glasgow. He is the author of six poetry collections including his most recent, Greengown: New and Selected Poems (Carcanet, 2022). He initiated and co-edited the poetry magazine, Verse, with Robert Crawford and Henry Hart in the 1980s, is a founder and past Chair of The Edwin Morgan Trust and helped to establish the Scottish Writers' Centre. He won a Cholmondeley Award in 2022 in recognition of his work to date and is Professor Emeritus of Poetry at the University of Strathclyde.

POEM

David Wheatley

INTERIOR WITH INTERIOR
(Pieter Neefs, Interior of Antwerp Cathedral)

It is dark in the castle; it is
bright in the church. Antwerp Cathedral
in Crathes Castle, here in the bed-
room. What travellers we have been, in
our time. It is a fungible world,
the cool still-life with a lobster and
ham: commodities not essences.
The church as repository of
empty space in a cluttered world, the
light of the Renaissance gone for a
walk in the street and spilling slantways
over the nave where a pair of dogs
have paused between a beggar and priest.
But secular, this archive of air,
less aura and halo than glaze and
sheen, and here among the tombs life takes
refuge where a woman sinks into
the tulip bulb of her dress to breast-
feed an almost invisible child.
I find there are several versions.
At a certain close remove from the
original a copy or a
copy of a copy becomes an
original again, and what you
are seeing is where your gaze comes to
rest inside the gaze of the other.
As he was dying Ciaran Carson
entered afresh the world of Golden
Age Dutch-Flemish art, projecting one

thing onto another, as one might
Holland onto Ireland or Scotland:
studied the course of decay via
an orange he watched turn greeny-blue;
the light had only to fall this way
or that on the tiles for a Metsu
postcard on the wall to fill the room
and repeat itself in the here and
now. On looking into it further
I notice the figures gathered in
Neef's foreground vary from version to
version, circulating between them
as bustlingly as we move from room
to room under the corbelled corner
turrets, their crones' teeth of bartizans
and bretasches snagged on the hem of
the sky. The destruction of the Queen
Anne wing in a fire means we pass from
present to the Renaissance with no
intermediary stage. Time lords
it benevolently over us
where a twist of the pepper-mill stairs
shakes us back a random century.
Fancy though stepping out of one frame
only to find another outside
it, baffling yet liberating at
once. Wandering downstairs from the Neefs
we enter the muses' room, with on
the ceiling all nine storied sisters
(Euterpe I am, this arte did found…)
undulating over the beams, a
shade too enthusiastically
repainted in Victorian times.
Twang goes a clarsach string our son plucks.
It is debatable whether the
Reformation, since we are talking
about the Reformation, truly
took in these parts. Now ask me what the

POEM: DAVID WHEATLEY

Baronet and the Marquess discussed
over wine in 1644
while the warhorses waited outside
impatient for things to be cleared up,
to be on the move. A cloudless night
brings clarity, and not forgetting
Urania as we leave, a globe
in her hand subsuming castle and
church, patron of the harsh scatter of
stars traced in braille above the river.

See biographical on p 138.

POEM

Rob McClure

AIRDRIE

I miss it
not at all
recalling sleeted rain and a razorblade
wind looted trees and skelped kiddies
weeping on monkey bars
as peloothered alkies exited theirs
staggering and spewing
profanity, brandishing broken bottlenecks,
flick-knives, sharper carpet-cutters,
fancying a nice chip poke from Neta's
and sporadic paraffin-blue skies gave
terrible light to freckled summers

except (swithering) maybe

that one time just
us up on the Old Town Cross
crucified for a greased fish supper,
by the dripping chicken rotisserie
of Zambonini's café la fiesta,
you ponytailing lovely night,
and asking me for another light
(and you all the light there was!),
steam thrilling from a grate intrigued
your bare white legs and you shimmy-
giggled like a dream of chocolate
(pink ribbon, pink ribbon!)
and my heart leapt out of me

Rob McClure is an expatriate Scot currently working in Illinois. He has published quite widely in the United States (in journals including Chicago Quarterly Review, Gettysburg Review *and* New Ohio Review). *Over the past few years, he has tended homeward, with poetry appearing in* Poetry Scotland, New Writing Scotland, Lallans, Eeemus Stane *and* Dreich. *He has published fiction in* Gutter, Chapman, *and the* Manchester Review *and has had a collection of fiction,* The Violence, *published by Queen's Ferry Press in the US. His novel* The Scotsman *won the Black Springs Detective Fiction Prize and came out in 2023.*

POEM

Ryan Van Winkle

CITY SNOWPRINTS, 2018

It got late. I took a snow day.
I took a walk. There had been
a lot of giving that winter.

I was becoming a stool
in a bar where everyone
had gone home. It felt like

even the lights
were spending the season
with their wives and kids.

Sure, I thought I'd be happy
in the dark. Welcome the sky
full of static again.

I imagined kids rolling
a snowman in a parking lot.
But at night I only found

footprints and claw prints
aimless and random,
all crossed over with bicycle tracks.

The pavement offered no crumbs to the birds.
I thought, I should take a rest, stop giving a shit
what the lights aren't doing. They gum you up,

they do. Imagine a carrot instead,
the dog snatching it like a bone.

Ryan Van Winkle is an American poet based in Edinburgh for over 20 years. His second collection, The Good Dark, *won the Saltire Society's 2015 Poetry Book of the Year award. His poems have appeared in* The American Poetry Review, Modern Poetry in Translation, The Edinburgh Review *and* New Writing Scotland. *His third collection is forthcoming from Polygon.*

POEM

Morag Smith

AN ISLAND SPEAKS TO ITS CASTLE

My volcano could have told you; memory
built on lava, Gabbros, Peridotites
knows woodlands scoured bare will still be more
than a rich man's playground. Your back was always turned
to watch worlds disembark at the pier
for Edwardian plumbing and fresh grown figs.

Leather boots crush pennycress and sandwort, matchstick men
with guns pose for the camera, workmen paid to wear kilts
feel on their skin oceanic gales they know will salt
and rot and in the summer, Lady Monica perspires,
in the fetid air of her "Salon Parissienne", listening
to the tap tap of many-eyed swarms on mullioned glass.

Kilmory's skeleton phone box twitters with coal tits
and chaffinch. Kittiwakes and Razorbills, call
from the Cuillin, telling you not to be afraid.
Lichens embrace your crumbling steps, mosses soothe
wind-scarred cloisters and at 3 a.m., the laird's
orchestrion creaks and whistles, food for woodworms
– nothing will be wasted.

(Kinloch castle is on the island of Rùm, in the Inner Hebrides)

Morag Smith lives in Paisley and was brought up in working-class Glasgow. Her poetry has been published in e-zines, magazines and anthologies, including Scottish Poetry Library Best Scottish Poems of 2023, Paperboats.org, Poetry Ireland Review, The Scotsman *and* Gutter. *She is the winner of the 2021 Paisley Book Festival/Janet Coates Memorial Poetry Prize; and was shortlisted for the Ginkgo Ecopoetry Prize in 2021 and for the Bridport Poetry Prize in 2022. Her first pamphlet,* Background Noises, *published by Red Squirrel Press in 2022, concerns the human and ecological history of a semi-derelict psychiatric hospital in Renfrewshire.*

POEM

Finola Scott

THOSE LAUNDS

let's consideer those launds   the you tak the high road
     launds   words rage fir years
hunders ride oot tae scance herrins broddit tae
     bannocks thon gaunt streetch-shift
on buses hurtlin unner sundoun thae A'll tak the low
     roads nae hieroglyphics jist
ferries nae sailing cars hurtling oan motorway   mort
     kist roads and drove roads   the
history o Gaeldom whispert by names o railwey
     stations   thae saltire signs braw lads
all plunner forgat   the Reivers' skeichit cattle tuckit
     unner a fingernail muin
sauf lairit in the Devil's Beeftub flesh smouderin
     history re-re-re branded   John
McLean forgot miners forgot drugs ignored oor young
     forgot whiles salmon bide
oan ferms cod are swept up wi machines hunners
     march tae change things   but
naethin changes aye greedy talk of oil aneath the oor
     watter

this laund   inatween rivers   oor dwamfle space
     demarked by Romans — twice —
they did likit thir waws   roads and cesses   forbye a
     wee bath   nae Mason or Dixon
nae Cyril Radcliffe   insteid warfare gangs on —
     submarines slide aroond the lochs

thither and yon   yon and thither   the laund burst o the
            Tweed lapperin   let's lat licht
fir the doorway sleepers   unco loss   thoosands
            hameless   bairns hungry   ootside
food banks   whiles the sign cries   *People Make Glasgow*

blithe lads and lassies   slippit oer   thon threapit ratch on
            the map   ablow the wind ferms
stirrin the lift   tae bind thegither   an anvil bricht ringin
            thair trowhs   hame   shortbreid
broth and bridies   fir them in twa capped families   the
            routine cheerin o haibit   in the
keek o day birdiesang   bygangin thon hailsin saltire
            thon braw   summer-blue sign
at the Mairches   aback-seat bairns sooking on tablet
            thon man who would walk five
hundred miles mair   aye weel   he mun tae find wurk   or
            deek an osprey   thae hauf mindi
hauf mummlet sangs   the haste-ye-back elaskit   o kith
            and kin   that binds us still thgither
maks us forget the auld folk   biding cauld at hame   or
            stuck in hospitals   the green belt
eelit   sic a scunner   aw the lies and cheatrie we
            mun swallie   ach whae's like us?!

Finola Scott's work is widely published in magazines and anthologies such as New Writing Scotland, Gutter, One Hand Clapping, The Ofi Press *and* Lighthouse. *Mentored on the Clydebuilt Scheme by the poet Liz Lochhead, she has been writing since retiring from a life at the chalk face.*

TO MAKE YOUR VERY OWN DÙN

Alec Finlay with Ken Cockburn

you will require:

twin peaks, one always
  higher than the other
    with the dùn on the lower

a conspectus over
  moorland or plain, toward
    a screen of mountains

a geomantic alignment
  with cup-and-ring marked rocks
    and standing stones

a *hosomichi* or small winding path,
  usually obscured by fern or heather,
    and a spring or well

a mythic figure
  whether Saint, King, Warrior
    Cailleach, Witch or Seer

a tale, always tragic –
  traditionally
    no dùn has a happy ending

a disputed association
  with the Stone of Destiny
    or with a replica

(by which is meant
  a real replica
    and not a fake)

sorrel, wild thyme, foxgloves,
  with always a rowan
    secure at the margin

and for those who wish
  to stay alert,
    a distant hill and rival dùn.

Alec Finlay (born 1966, Scotland) is a poet and artist whose work crosses over a range of media and forms. In 2020 he was awarded a Cholmondeley Award for services to poetry. He recently completed I remember: Scotland's Covid Memorial. *Publications include* I remember *(2022),* descriptions *(2022),* a far-off land *(2018), and* gathering *(2018). A selected shorter poems,* play my game, *was published by Stewed Rhubarb in 2023.*

Ken Cockburn is a poet and translator based in Edinburgh who works in education, care and community settings, and often collaborates with visual artists. He also runs Edinburgh Poetry Tours, guided walks with readings of poems in the city's Old Town. Recent publications with The Caseroom Press include Edinburgh: poems & translations, Wale *and* Scenes from Otherwise Forgotten Films.

FROM THE SCOTTISH ARCHIVE

SCOTTISH CULTURE AND THE END OF BRITAIN (2002)

Angus Calder

May the era of Henderson begin.

I'm writing in the aftermath of two big Scottish deaths.

Hamish Henderson was an astonishing figure, central to Scottish cultural development from World War II on, and crucial to the achievement of our new Parliament in 1999. Out of his service in North Africa with the 51st Highland Division came *Elegies for the Dead in Cyrenaica*. This sequence, with its learning, reflection and passion challenges comparison with the biggest men of Modernist verse in these islands – Yeats, Eliot, MacDiarmid. It was at once recognised as a startling achievement, making poetic sense out of a terrible war. But Hamish also emerged as the balladeer of the 8th Army and in the '50s he was the major collector and scholar of the Scottish Folk Revival. This had immense political implications, and Hamish expressed in song as well as in prose his detestation of nuclear weapons, imperialism and racism and his non-sectarian Marxist socialism.

Since he was a republican, it must seem odd to set him beside Elizabeth Bowes Lyon, born in Glamis Castle near Forfar, who became Queen of Britain and co-head of the British Empire (which she most certainly didn't oppose). But her "common touch" which helped to rally Britain in the dark days of Blitz clearly stemmed from a Scottish environment where her father, Earl of Strathmore, had the time of day for every tenant; and after George VI's death she baffled her English courtiers by choosing to acquire Mey Castle in Caithness, a county notable not for "lovely" glens apt for the persecution of grouse and stags but for bracing winds, stark wee cliffs facing cold dangerous seas, heelstergowdie cloods and dour folk. (After she died, a couple of these courtiers turned up on TV admitting how much they'd hated it, and I fell about laughing ...) History moves on. She was as Scottish as Hamish. But her year was 1940. His was 1999.

"British" as a word defining cultural identity was always of restricted application and is now terminally infirm. But it has served a valuable end, heuristically, in defining and marshalling at certain junctures – the

Battle of Waterloo, the Battle of Britain — the commitment of people from various parts of the island to a common cause. In both cases, "liberty" was on the agenda.

Since sport matters more than politics to a high proportion of the populations of these islands, I'll begin considering Scotland and Britain historically from that perspective then move back to songs, remembering Fletcher of Saltoun's remark that "if a man were permitted to make all the ballads, he need not care who should make the laws of a nation".

The rules of many sports were codified in Britain in the 19th century. Accordingly the first international contests in association and rugby football were between teams from different parts of the British Isles. Interesting anomalies result from this. Five teams from the islands are allowed to compete in European and World Cup soccer competitions. In Rugby Union, the arrival of the Irish Free State in 1922 did not disrupt the practice of selecting Irish rugby teams from both South and North, including Protestants alongside Catholics. Touring in the Southern Hemisphere, the best Irish players have been happy to represent the "British" Lions. Since the First World War, the Five Nations championship has brought together teams from all the territories once claimed by Plantagenet and Tudor monarchs.

In Scotland, unlike Wales, Rugby Union was the "people's game" only in the Borders. Elsewhere, like the south of England, it had a small base consisting chiefly of men educated in fee-paying schools, and soccer was dominant as the sport, effectively the religion, of the Lowland Scottish masses. Nevertheless, rugby internationals attracted huge crowds. There were surges of national pride in 1984 and 1990 when Scotland, with the smallest pool of players, beat the other four nations to achieve the Grand Slam. On the second occasion, captain David Sole famously terrified his opponents in the shootout at Murrayfield, when the English also might have achieved a Grand Slam, by leading his team out in a slow march rather than the usual brisk gallop as the crowd howled out the recently composed anthem "Flower of Scotland". Around the Millennium, each other nation in turn, as if in conspiracy, denied England four successive Grand Slams.

English fans, like their TV commentators, are not noted for their sense of humour. They find Celtic solidarity against them rather upsetting. They are dismayed by the fact that Scots tend to support anyone, including Iraq, Botswana, Fiji or North Korea, competing against any English team internationally, whether at football, cricket, or tiddlywinks. "But we always support *your* sides," they whine, before the more erudite of them, who read *The*

Guardian (which covers Scottish affairs especially badly) digress into their fantasy that ethnic cleansing of the English will occur if Scotland ever votes for independence. But ethnicity has nothing to do with it ...

The fact is that no sane Scot believes that there is a Scottish "race"; or anything which could be defined as a Scottish "ethnicity". Geographically, Scotland has the most stable borders in Europe, identical since the 1470s, when the Northern Isles were acquired from Denmark. The population was of diverse Welsh Brythonic, Irish Gaelic, Pictish and Anglo-Saxon stock. When some of us set up the Scottish Poetry Library in 1984 we announced our intention to include verse in all "the three leids" of Scotland – Scots, Gaelic and English. I have since come to think that one could argue that Scotland has more than three languages, since North Eastern Doric and Norse-based Shetlandic might claim as much autonomy as Portuguese has from Spanish, leaving aside the distinctive patois of Glasgow, Lothian and Fife, which might be considered mere dialects.

Cultural differences related to this are so pronounced that one could imagine Scotland dissolving, along lines favoured by Fletcher of Saltoun himself, into a set of city states within the expanded European Union. Recently, after she gave a reading in Edinburgh, I put up my friend Sheena Blackhall from Aberdeen, the leading writer of poetry and stories in Aberdeenshire Doric and also a fine unaccompanied singer in the tradition of the travelling people. Visiting Shetland she detected great prejudice against Aberdeen, which has functioned as a metropolis for those islands. People there preferred their close cousins, Norwegian trawlermen to crews from the Northeast of Scotland. She has found that the Doric is in steep decline in its historic rural heartland. The peasant culture of the Northeast has waned since the cataclysm of the First World War, and now incomers, often English, have been attracted to work in and around the North Sea oil industry. So, in rustic Aberdeenshire, English and Anglicised speech have gained ground, and the epicentre of Doric is now found in working class areas of Aberdeen itself, reversing the former pattern. Anyway, after the success on TV of *Rab C Nesbitt* and of the film of *Trainspotting*, young people regard Glaswegian or Leith patter as cool, whereas Doric is old-fashioned.

However, Sheena would agree that Scots language(s) will survive. Apart from the rich body of literature produced from the middle ages onwards in various forms of Scots, the country has the strongest tradition of folk-song in Western Europe. The status of Burns as cardinal national hero, and the rituals of Burns Night are significant. So is the Folksong Revival led in the 1950s by

Hamish Henderson and Norman Buchan. Henderson moved around Scotland recording non-professional singers while Buchan and others were vividly interested in songs to traditional tunes as a motor of up-to-date radical politics. Songs old and new, in any and every version of spoken Scots, passed from singer to singer, accompanied CND marches and helped to inspire the turn of fortune which in the late '60s transformed the SNP from a fringe organisation of eccentrics into a major contender in local and national politics. Music can be said to provide a surrogate for an otherwise indefinable "Scottish identity". This provides reassurance that a multi-ethnic, multi-cultural Scotland can work, in so far as immigrants from Europe, Asia and Africa have adapted to and added to the Scottish repertoire of entertainment. I know personally a performance poet whose father was a Yoruba coalminer in Cowdenbeath and a singer called Andy, also from Fife, who looks like a full-blooded Polynesian but will belt out "Scots Wha Hae" with the best of them.

As they pick up Scottish mindsets, such people are less and less likely to think of themselves as British. A survey published towards the end of 2001 revealed that 37% of Scots now consider themselves to be Scottish not British compared with 19% in 1992. Asked to make a straight choice in 1992, 57% affirmed that they were Scottish rather than British – in 2001 80% decided to be Scottish (*The Times*, 17 December, 2001). One will still encounter people who reject what they conceive to be a parochial Scottish identity in favour of being British. But their numbers seem set to dwindle, despite low support for independence – the SNP in opinion polls only very rarely attract more than a third of the electorate – and lack of much enthusiasm for the performance of the new Scottish Parliament.

The late '60s were when the hinge was swung. The Folksong Revival intersected with the end of the British Empire. Colony after colony was relinquished. Young Scots who would formerly have looked forward to employment under the Union Jack overseas now had to consider their chances in their homeland. Meanwhile, "nationalism" was in fashion all over the world as ex-colonial countries experimented with independence. Minority rights were an important issue. Beside the surge of Black Power in the USA and the Civil Rights movement in Northern Ireland, Basques and Catalans in Spain, Bretons and Occitanians in France, Sardinians in Italy, were seeking political clout. Left-wing activists joined the SNP from the marching ranks of the Campaign for Nuclear Disarmament, and electoral success began with Winnie Ewing's famous by-election victory over Labour in Hamilton in 1967. The exploitation of oil in North Sea waters gave the SNP a specious slogan

– "It's Scotland's Oil" – just as the great postwar world boom was ended by the muscle-flexing of oil producing countries in 1973. In Westminster 0seats and share of the vote the SNP hit its all-time peak in 1974, since when it has settled down almost as a regional party in Northeast Scotland, but that success spurred Labour towards producing a weak devolution bill which failed in the 1979 Referendum yet gave Home Rule a place on the left's political agenda.

Meanwhile, there is general agreement that Scottish culture had entered a remarkable period. Scottish writers, artists and musicians related themselves directly to developments in Europe and America; English culture seemed tame and unfocussed in comparison. It can be said that this newly assured sense of cultural distinctiveness converged with the "democratic deficit" established in the 1980s, when Thatcher's government was deeply antipathetic to most Scots. Gradually voted out of Scotland, the Tory party nevertheless continued to impose its policies, with the Secretary of State looking more and more like a colonial Viceroy attempting to subdue fractious natives. The Tories were wiped out in local government in 1995 and lost every Scottish seat at Westminster in the 1997 General Election, after which the Blair Government simply had to accede to the settled will of the Scottish people.

Paradoxically, there seems to be growing consensus among historians that the Scottish "nation" which now seems to be established, like Catalonia, as a distinctive component of the new Europe, originates historically in and through the Parliamentary Union with England in 1707 which gave Scots the chance to achieve prosperity as collaborators in the British Empire.

To accept, or swallow, this proposition, one has to distinguish between the medieval meaning of "nation", applying simply to people coming from a certain geographical space and sharing quasi-familial bonds, and the modern sense of the word, implying "nation state", which supersedes the old sense of the word "empire", as when James VI & I asserted that Britain – the island he now ruled – was an "empire", meaning a noteworthy expanse of territory under a single powerful sovereign. Scotland before 1707 was the Kingdom of the King of Scots, who since 1603 had been King of England also. Its parliament met intermittently and had established no significant traditions of debate or lawmaking, its bureaucracy was sketchy, judicial power was devolved to local magnates whose rights were secured by a chaotic mixter-maxter of feudal laws.

Scots anticipated the thrust towards popular representative government which was consummated in the American and French Revolutions in the

Declaration of Arbroath of 1320. Scottish barons assured the Pope, firstly, that they followed Robert Brus as their King, as against Edward of England, and secondly that if Brus betrayed the Scottish interest at some future date they would depose him. This right to depose unjust rulers was reaffirmed by John Knox and George Buchanan, in the name of the common people, at the time of the Scottish Reformation when the new Protestant Church of Scotland might have become, as in England, the basis of an emergent nation state. But it didn't. Presbyterians opposed the attempts of Stuart Kings to establish bishops as agents of royal control. Landed magnates joined them in the National Covenant of 1637 when Charles I attempted to anglicise the forms of the Church of Scotland along with its organisation. After this movement fell apart in the late 1640s, Scotland became easy prey for Cromwell's army, which established by force such centralised rule as Scotland had never previously experienced. Something like an emergent modern "nation" can be seen after the Restoration of Stuart rule in 1660, with a great systematisation of Scots Law, a role for the Scottish Parliament in economic affairs, and developments, largely inspired by the achievements of Calvinist Holland, which prepared the way for intellectual Enlightenment and agricultural improvement in the next century. The establishment of a Presbyterian Church of Scotland after the fall of James VII & II in 1689 was a further step towards coherent modernisation. But the collapse of Scottish aspirations to an independent overseas trading empire with the abortive Darien project of the 1690s helped ensure that arguments for Parliamentary Union with England prevailed with the ruling elite in 1707, when the Scottish Parliament voted itself out of existence. Scotland emerged as modern nation in the 18th century.

Scotland retained a distinctive national church, and independent legal and educational systems. European contemporaries deeply impressed with Scottish achievements in thought, science and literature easily saw that these were not "English" and indeed the prowess of Hume, Smith, Macpherson and Burns was definitely not a product of the Union. These men and other pioneers in thought and culture drew strength from distinctive Scottish traditions traceable back to much earlier centuries. In return for supplying parliamentary votes *en bloc* to whichever government held sway at Westminster, the "managers" of Scotland – first the Dukes of Argyll, then the Earl of Bute, then, most successfully of all, the canny Lothian lawyer Henry Dundas – controlled patronage in Scotland and governed the country as much as its influential people thought it needed. By this means the old power of the regional magnates adapted to the new politics.

Middling Scots on the make swarmed into England's overseas colonies and trading posts, taking over whole sugar islands in the West Indies, seizing control of the Virginia tobacco trade, the Canadian fur trade, and establishing from the 1720s onwards a wholly disproportionate stake in the successes and rich spoils of the East India Company in India. The fortunes brought back by Scottish merchants, administrators, soldiers and sailors furthered the agricultural improvement of what had been an habitually half-starved country and fuelled sudden industrial revolution, with the help of rich local deposits of coal and oil-shale. Highlands and Islands were opened up to modern economic development. Walter Scott projected the romantic history of his homeland to the delight and astonishment of the Western World, not forgetting All-the-Russias and modernising native élites in India. But it was now the most up-to-date of all nations, its scope extended by the conquests of the British and Indian Armies backed by the omnipotent Royal Navy, for which the Clyde came to supply ships while South Wales provided the steam coal. Scottish capital was rampant in spheres as far apart as the tea and opium trades of China and cattle ranching in the USA's Wild West. By 1900, Glasgow was a model for the modern city and Scotland was probably the richest country in the world.

Linda Colley has demonstrated, in her seminal book *Britons*, how the idea of Britishness came to prevail between the Union of 1707 and the accession of Victoria in 1837. The long series of conflicts between Britain and France, between the great Protestant sea power and the big continental Catholic military power, forged the invention of Britishness. A Scottish poet, James Thomson, wrote the words of "Rule Britannia". Britons, whether English, Welsh or Scottish, defined themselves, as Colley puts it, "... against the French as they imagined them to be, superstitious, militarist, decadent and unfree. And, increasingly, as the wars went on, they defined themselves in contrast to the colonial peoples they conquered, peoples who were manifestly alien in terms of culture, religion and colour." Even some Irish Catholics became British patriots, before and after the Union of the Irish Parliament with Westminster in 1800. But the cultures of the archipelago did not blend. As Walter Scott showed, one could preserve the most intense passion for Caledonia stern and wild, one's own, one's native land, while rejoicing in the triumphs of the British armed forces over Napoleon and expressing devout loyalty to the Hanoverian dynasty which, despite the madness of George III and the profligacy of his son and heir, had come to represent for Britons not only the virtues of sturdy monarchy under the sublime British Constitution, but, most improbably, family values.

The climax of the new Scottish combination of innovation, prosperity and small-n nationalism with proud acceptance of British identity came in the era of Scott and Byron, when Scottish thought and literature awed Europe, Edinburgh vied as a centre of publishing with London and Paris, and successive British prime ministers – Melbourne, Palmerston and Russell – studied at Edinburgh University. This didn't last.

The death of Scott in 1832 coincided with the departure of Thomas Carlyle to London, the development of the railway and the reform of national and local government which destroyed Scotland's oligarchic system. Though Edinburgh still had many decades ahead of it as a major centre of publishing, Scottish writers now sought fame in London. The railway drastically reduced travelling times between Scotland and the south-east of England. In the 18th century not one English man had represented a Scottish parliamentary seat (though many Scots had been elected in England). Now prominent English parliamentarians found constituencies north of the border. The triumphant liberalism of free trade, with its dehumanised version of Adam Smith's political economy, had no time for romantic nationalist ideas. Scotland might as well be "North Britain", as many of its people came to style it as they addressed letters adorned with stamps which did not mention Britain at all, as they still don't.

Early in Victoria's reign, the term "British Empire" still referred primarily to the United Kingdom of Great Britain and Ireland. "Imperialism" was a nasty thing which boastful French popinjays indulged in. By the time the old queen died, it was the proud creed of most Tories and many Liberals; she herself had been created Empress of India by her clever prime minister Disraeli. Half-baked Scottish nationalism in the 20th century would put it about that England, having subordinated Scotland and in some sense "colonised" it, sent the country's active males out into the worldwide Empire to do its dirty work as policemen, soldiers and administrative and professional dogsbodies with the connivance of a Scottish upper class deracinated by attendance at English public boarding schools.

That in every part of the Empire Scots were prominent and important surely belies this caricature. In some – the economy, culture and politics of Canada, African exploration and missions, Bengal jute, Hong Kong banking and trade with China – Scots were quite simply dominant. Michael Fry, in his important book *Scottish Empire* (2001) has argued forcibly that Scots used the empire for their own ends. They were not interested in acquiring vast new territories but in commercial profit and social improvement, at home and overseas. Coincidentally Martha McLaren, a Canadian scholar, in a study of *British India and British Scotland* (Akron, Ohio 2001) has emphasised the importance of their origins in the Scottish Enlightenment of three administrators whose doctrines and practices had a cardinal influence on the development of the British Raj in India – Thomas Munro, John Malcolm and Mountstuart Elphinstone. They were not, as previous historians saw them, conservatives of the Edmund Burke school – "... they required land tenure and revenue collection systems that encouraged rather than inhibited progress; they required the creation of economically and politically active 'middling' social groups to function as the agents of improvement; and they required, as a counterpoise to the inevitably authoritarian nature of imperial rule, liberty for Indians to participate in the administration, if not the legislation, of their own country – particularly the administration of justice." Both Fry and McLaren reinforce the view put forward some years ago by John Mackenzie, Professor of Imperial History at the University of Lancaster, that a distinctive "Scottish social ethos" informed the activities of prominent Scots in the Empire exemplified, for instance, by David Livingstone.

Livingstone thought that poor Scots would gain from emigrating to central Africa – but believed that local Africans wherever these emigrants settled would be brought as equals into the modern world by trading with Scots and learning from them. When presenting himself to English and European people in Africa, Livingstone was happy to call himself "English". When writing about his dreams and schemes to fellow-countryman Sir Roderick Murchison, head of the Royal Geographical Society in London, he reverted to being a patriotic Scot. I think such double identity was characteristic of Victorian Scots. It went along with Carlyle's notion that the English were great doers but needed others – presumably Scots like himself – to perform their thinking for them and with the smug conviction, rarely voiced in public, that the Empire was really run by Scots.

It was a Scottish politician, Lord Rosebery, who first, in the 1880s, put forward the idea of a British "Commonwealth of Nations". This re-emerged after a disastrous Great War in which troops from White Dominions had acquitted themselves most notably; its presence in Scottish debate in the 1920s has been generally overlooked. No one could miss the enthusiasm of Scotland's leading intellectual imperialist, John Buchan, for the white Dominions. It went along with a passionate attachment to Scots language and strong sympathy for Scottish Home Rule. Hence his encouragement of MacDiarmid's project to promote a new Scottish Renaissance in the arts.

If the Great War was a calamitous watershed for Britain as a whole, it hit Scotland particularly hard. Through the Scottish regiments, used as shock troops and in forlorn-hope actions, the country suffered the heaviest per capita casualty rate in Western Europe – one has to go as far east as Serbia to match it. Scottish heavy industry – coal, engineering, shipbuilding, iron and steel – had a spasm of climactic activity. Then after the war export markets dwindled or disappeared. In a spate of nationalistic thinking, related to the appearance – within the Commonwealth, be it remembered, until 1949 – of the Irish Free State, the idea that Scotland should have Home Rule as a Dominion, equal in status to Canada, Australia and Eire, commended itself for a time even to such an extremist as MacDiarmid.

The emergence in 1927 of the National Party of Scotland which MacDiarmid co-founded, and which became the Scottish National Party in the 1930s, was a natural outcome in a period which saw a Constitutional Convention in Scotland involving Liberal, Labour and non-party elements, the failure of several Home Rule bills, and the creation, by public subscription, of the magnificent Scottish National War Memorial on Castle Hill, Edinburgh – a direct result of the Duke of Atholl's angry response during the war when an English MP had suggested a British National Memorial in Hyde Park. This was formally opened in 1927. The popular writer whose pseudonym was Ian Hay, formerly Major Beith of the Argyll and Sutherland Highlanders, proclaimed in a souvenir book that "Scotland alone among the nations has erected a National War Memorial commemorating in detail the service of every unit of her Arms, and the name of every one of her hundred thousand dead" (*Their Name Liveth*, 1931). Hay underestimates casualties greatly, but his point is clear. Along with other right-wing Scots he wanted to celebrate the special military sacrifice of a very special nation. I'm sure Elizabeth Bowes Lyon went along with that.

What sidelined this nationalist upsurge was the great slump of 1929–1931, which came near to wholly destroying what was left of Scottish heavy industry in a period, furthermore, of severe agricultural depression. Scotland in 1914 had been a proud and wealthy co-partner in the Greatest Empire the World Had Ever Seen. In the '30s, high unemployment persisted even while the Southeast and Midlands of England made a sparkling recovery through the new light engineering industries. Daunted and demoralised, Scots began to blame the English for their troubles, and a tradition of whinge began which sadly persists in some quarters to the present day. Meanwhile, however, the Scottish Office was devolved from Whitehall to that huge new building on

Edinburgh's Calton Hill, so that in a sense, up to a point, the government of Scotland came home to Scotland.

In Churchill's wartime Coalition Government, the Secretary of State for Scotland was Tom Johnston. This left wing veteran of the Red Clyde had promoted in the '30s the London Scots Self Government Committee, creating the impression that the Labour Party favoured Home Rule. Johnston himself was unquestionably a patriot, and used the then-fictitious bogey of rampant Scottish Nationalism to persuade Churchill to let him introduce, through quangos and by administrative fiat, striking reforms in his homeland even in wartime. Labourites were duly convinced that administrative devolution was enough. The senile arteries of Scottish heavy industry were flooded again with war contracts, it staggered to its feet and unluckily kept going after 1945, aided by the subsidies to regions handed out by Labour and Tory governments. Scottish nationhood reached a nadir in 1955, when over 50% percent of the electorate voted Conservative, followed a few years later by the Labour Party's abandonment of a traditional commitment to Home Rule which dated back to Keir Hardie.

This is easily explained. The heroic and successful war created a new focus for pride in Britishness. Scots had served alongside fellow-Britons in the armed forces, and Scottish females had flooded south to work in English centres of war industry, often marrying Englishmen. The populations of the island had been scrambled together as never before. Full employment and handouts from Westminster afterwards mitigated anti-English grievance. The unravelling of Britishness commenced only in the 1960s.

In a very simple way Scots must always be British, since we mostly live on an island called Britain. Our bit of it was never purely British ethnically, since the Brythonic Celts occupied only the south of Scotland. However, Scotland, even Orkney, featured in "the Matter of Britain", the body of Arthurian legends stabilised by Geoffrey of Monmouth in the 12th century. Recent studies by Robert Crawford and others have emphasised the great, even dominant influence of Scottish writers on English literature since the 18th century, but only an idiot could fail to notice that Robert Burns idolised Alexander Pope and that Scott's momentous achievements in fiction drew on those of Shakespeare and the English Restoration dramatists, as well as the novels of Defoe, Richardson and Fielding. For that matter, sorting out – as Michael Fry has tried to do – a distinctive Scottish presence in the Victorian Empire will always be complicated, if not sabotaged, by the very success of Scottish Enlightenment thinking south of the Border, producing Anglo-Scottish, or if you like, "British" ideological soups. Both John Stuart Mill and John Ruskin had Scottish parents and would always have been fully qualified to play soccer or rugby for Scotland, but to claim that their thought is "Scottish" would be pettily chauvinistic.

I return to sport, where I began. It illustrates surviving anomalies and contradictions. Scotland, along with the Channel Islands and the Isle of Man, has its own representation in the Commonwealth Games, but its competitors become British, if picked, in the Olympics, even when they are curlers, adept in a sport not practised at all south of the Border. Any Westminster politician wishing to ensure that Scotland immediately declares full independence will seriously follow up and enforce somehow the idea put forward a few years ago by a temporarily insane Labour Sports Minister that there should be an All-British football team. Scotland will never give up the right to beat San Marino and draw with Faeroe in World Cup and European competition. But our biggest teams, Rangers and Celtic, want to play in the English Premier Division...

Only a huge political upheaval involving violence will unite the Basques of Spain and France in a single homeland. The people of Catalonia, we are told, like the Spanish better now that they have achieved a substantial measure of Home Rule and are mostly content to be Spanish as well as Catalan. Such notable historical entities as Brittany, Flanders and Bavaria, now merely regions or *länder*, are incorporated into a European Union which will probably soon include independent countries – Latvia and Slovenia – which had not the merest ghost of existence before the twentieth century and others – the Czech Republic, Poland, Lithuania and Hungary – whose present boundaries have been arbitrarily determined by the outcomes of appallingly brutal wars. "Scotland in Europe" has been a recent SNP slogan. In so far as Scotland is and always has been a European country, this gets one no further than "Scotland in Britain" would. In so far as it points to the same status as Denmark and Finland, countries of similar population, it implies no more, if no less, independence "in Europe" than these currently enjoy. Since England has ten times as many people as Scotland, democracy insists that it will always weigh more in Europe.

Two decades ago, when I was editing an anthology of 20th century poetry in English from Britain for a publisher in the old East Germany, she insisted that it had to be called *Englische Lyrik*. Her argument was that Britain is a merely bureaucratic concept, like "European Union". Right enough – the *Wehrmacht* in 1940 sang that they were marching "against England", not Britain. The only context in which the adjective British had cultural, rather than just bureaucratic significance, was in the terms "British Army" (but note – Royal Navy and Royal Air Force) and "British Empire". Recently attempts have been made to use British and Briton as words to incorporate recent immigrant groups – as in "British Asians" and "Black Britons". But black footballers born in England insist that they are English and want to play for England, and the Scottish Sikhs who invented a Sikh Tartan for the new Millennium were subscribing to Scotland not to Britain.

The British Constitution, which is supposed to enshrine this great British tradition, is notoriously unwritten. I hope that Mr. Blunkett will give all of us, not just immigrants, the chance to swear an oath to register ourselves as citizens of Britain. As things stand I am not myself a citizen. I am a subject of Queen Elizabeth II of the United Kingdom of Great Britain and Northern Ireland – Queen Elizabeth I of Scotland, as it happens – which means that I am completely at the mercy of the sovereignty of the Crown-in-Parliament. Equipped with my rights as a citizen at last, I could use them, along with my hereditary liberty, while pursuing my aim of freeing Scotland from that sovereignty, as vigorously as Bruce defied the claims of Edward II, and consolidating a Scottish Republic.

If the British Monarchy had crumbled in 1936–1941, as it might well have done, a people, or rather, a set of peoples, amongst whom republicans were a tiny minority, might have fallen into confusion and demoralisation and caved in before Nazism. Elizabeth Bowes Lyon, clever and beautiful and genuinely sympathetic towards ordinary subjects, saved the monarchy, with all its symbolic potency. Born in 1942 to leftwing parents, I simply might not have come into existence without her. Without Hamish, his songs and their spirit it is hard to imagine how the almost indistinguishable political and cultural movements of the 1980s could have created the momentum for our new Parliament.

Now we need a new momentum, a new cultural movement which can focus the fact that Scotland is not basically about Tartan, as the inane creation of Tartan Day in New York seems to propose. But what are we "about"? We can't be "British" any more. I suggest that we are, as we always have been, "European", whether or not we are steered into ever-closer union within the EC, or, as an independent republic, decide to get out. What is our distinctiveness to be?

The era of MacDiarmid is over. May the era of Henderson begin. "Freedom come all ye" has the implication of full-blooded internationalism. Our population is falling, and ageing. We need young workers and fresh genes in our always-mongrel mixture. We should aim for a Scotland in which immigrants are welcome and every school is multicultural. I think the new movement must be towards getting it to help us destroy racism and promote new syntheses with whatever customs and cultural forms new Scots – from Kosovo, say, and Afghanistan, from Sierra Leone and Somalia – bring when they come to join us. Frankly, with a declining population and good economic prospects, Scotland could do with plenty of Asian and Eastern European immigrants just now, illegal if necessary.

Angus Lindsay Ritchie Calder (1942–2008) was a Scottish writer, historian, and poet. He was born into a prominent left-wing family in London from Scotland. Initially studying English Literature at King's College, Cambridge, he became interested in political history (PhD, University of Sussex, 1968) and wrote a landmark and highly celebrated study on Britain during the Second World War in 1969 entitled The People's War, *considered by many to be the definitive volume on Britain's war years. He subsequently wrote several other historical works but turned to literature and poetry and worked primarily as a writer, though often holding a number of university teaching positions. He was the author of five collections of poetry, most latterly* Colours of Grief *(Shoestring, 2022),* Dipa's Bowl *(Aark Arts, 2004) and* Sun Behind the Castle: Edinburgh Poems *(Luath, 2004). An unabashed socialist and nationalist, he was a prominent Scottish public intellectual during the 1970s, 1980s and 1990s.*

NEW FROM
THE IRISH PAGES PRESS

Dear Orson Welles & Other Essays

By Mark Cousins

In this wide-ranging, stylish and iconoclastic book, Cousins reflects on his prolific career in filmmaking, meditating on the actors, directors, films, writers and philosophers that have influenced him, as well as on other adventures in filmland and on creativity in general. From recollections of his childhood in Belfast to practical film-making advice for new directors, to the complexities of representing trauma on screen, this is a book that will captivate readers interested in both contemporary film and the history of cinema.

"The remarkable range and depth of his knowledge provides anyone who has a passion for film-making with exciting new thoughts and ideas. He brings to life his remarkable and prolific career, shaped as it is by the philosophers, writers, actors and films that have influenced him. A great read."

The Generalist

irishpages.org

NEW FROM
THE IRISH PAGES PRESS

—

Genocide in Gaza: Israel's Long War on Palestine
By Avi Shlaim

In this book Avi Shlaim places Israel's policy towards the Gaza Strip under an uncompromising lens. He argues that recurrent attacks – what Israeli generals chillingly call "mowing the lawn" – are the inevitable result of Zionist settler colonialism whose basic objective is the elimination of the native population. In this war, however, Israel has gone beyond land-grabbing and ethnic cleansing to commit the crime of all crimes – genocide.

> "*Clear, forthright and cogent,* Genocide in Gaza *is essential reading for both those who understand little of Palestine-Israel and those who have followed the unfolding horrors for decades. As a historian, Shlaim is meticulous, thoughtful and robust. As a person who has lived in three worlds — Iraqi, Israeli and British, with a Jewish religion and an Arab ethnicity — few understand it as well on a personal level. His political vision is clear-sighted, his ideal humane.*"
>
> Selma Dabbagh, *novelist and human rights lawyer*

irishpages.org